DICTIONARY WORDS

As you read this book, you will find that some words are darker black ink than others on the page. You should look up the meaning of these words in your dictionary, if you do not already know them.

OTHER TITLES IN THE SERIES

The Baby Party and other stories

F. SCOTT FITZGERALD

Retold by Stephen Waller
Series Editor Derek Strange

PENGUIN ENGLISH

PENGUIN ENGLISH

Published by the Penguin Group
Penguin Books Ltd, 27 Wrights Lane, London W8 5TZ, England
Penguin Books USA Inc., 375 Hudson Street, New York, New York 10014, USA
Penguin Books Australia Ltd, Ringwood, Victoria, Australia
Penguin Books Canada Ltd, 10 Alcorn Avenue, Toronto, Ontario, Canada M4V 3B2
Penguin Books (NZ) Ltd, 182–190 Wairau Road, Auckland 10, New Zealand

Penguin Books Ltd, Registered Offices: Harmondsworth, Middlesex, England

'Bernice Bobs her Hair' was first published in 1920, 'The Baby Party' was first published in 1925,
'A Short Trip Home' was first published in 1927 and 'The Bridal Party' was first published in
1930
This adaptation published in Penguin Books 1991
3 5 7 9 10 8 6 4 2

The moral right of the adapter and illustrator has been asserted

Illustrations by David Cuzik (David Lewis Illustrators)
Designed by D W Design Partnership Ltd

Printed in England by Clays Ltd, St Ives plc
Set in 11/14 pt Lasercomp Bembo

The Baby Party
and other stories

1

Saturday night was dance night. The bright, yellow light streaming from the windows of the little club house was visible half a mile away. People used to come and stand outside and look in through the windows and watch the dancing. On these Saturday nights the club house was like a little theatre. Chairs were arranged in a circle around the walls – this was the **balcony**. The balcony was full of mainly middle-aged ladies with sharp eyes and icy hearts. Their purpose was to criticize. Occasionally they showed admiration, but they never gave encouragement. It is well-known among ladies over thirty-five that when young people dance in the summertime, they dance with the very worst intentions in the world. These ladies know that if the dancing couples are not conscious of the stony eyes watching them from the balcony, some of them will start strange, modern dances in the corners; and the more popular, more dangerous, girls will sometimes be kissed in parked cars.

But this circle of critics is not close enough to the stage to see the actors' faces and hear the words that are spoken. They can only lift their eyebrows, make guesses and judge the events according to their own fixed ideas. They never really understand the changing, sometimes cruel world of the young. No, the only real audience, and the main actors too, are the young people that move to the African sound of Dyer's Dance Band.

There is a wide variety of ages and conditions in this crowd of young people – from sixteen-year-old Otis Ormonde, still a schoolboy, to G. Reece Stoddard, a Harvard law graduate;

from little Madeleine Hogue, still feeling uncomfortable with her hair arranged on top of her head, to Bessie MacRae, the oldest of the girls and still not married. This young crowd is not only the centre of the stage, but contains the only people who can really see what is going on.

With a bang the music stops. The couples smile, repeat 'la-de-da-da dum-dum', and then the sound of young **feminine** voices rises over the clapping.

A few young men were left standing alone in the middle of the dance-floor. They had been about to interrupt one of the dancing couples and ask the man for permission to dance with his girl, a permission that could not be refused. But before they could **cut in**, the music stopped. Disappointed, they wandered back to the walls.

Warren MacIntyre, a student at Yale, was one of those disappointed young men. He felt in his dinner-coat pocket for a cigarette and walked outside. Couples were seated at tables and the air was filled with laughter. He nodded here and there at those he knew. It was not a large city and everyone knew everyone else. There, for example, were Jim Strain and Ethel Demorest. They had been talking of getting married for three years. Everyone knew that as soon as Jim managed to keep a job for more than two months, she would marry him. But how bored they both looked. And Ethel sometimes wore a puzzled expression, as if she wondered how she had ever got into this situation.

Warren was nineteen and pitied those of his friends who had not gone East to college. But, like most boys, he spoke proudly about the girls of his city when he was away from it. There was Genevieve Ormonde, for example, a regular guest at dances, house-parties and football games at Princeton, Yale, Williams and Cornell. There was black-eyed Roberta Dillon, famous among her generation. And, of course, there was Marjorie Harvey with her pretty face and quick tongue.

Warren had grown up across the street from Marjorie and had been 'crazy about her' for a long time. Sometimes she seemed grateful for his attention. But she told him that she had given him a fair trial, and she had found that she did not love him. The proof was this: When she was away from him, she forgot him and went out with other boys. For Warren this was discouraging, especially because Marjorie had been away a lot on little trips all summer. And then throughout the month of August she had been visited by her cousin Bernice from Eau Claire, and it seemed impossible to see her alone. It was always necessary to find someone who would take care of Bernice. This was becoming more and more difficult.

Compared to Marjorie, Cousin Bernice was a disappointment. She was pretty, with long dark hair, but she was not a success at parties. Every Saturday night Warren danced a long dance with her in order to please Marjorie, but she always bored him.

'Warren' – a soft voice interrupted his thoughts. He turned and saw Marjorie beside him. She laid a hand on his shoulder and a warm feeling came over him.

'Warren,' she whispered, 'do something for me – dance with Bernice. She's been stuck with little Otis Ormonde for almost an hour.'

The warm feeling disappeared.

'Why – sure,' he answered weakly.

Marjorie smiled – that smile that was thanks enough. 'You're an angel.'

With a sigh the angel looked round, but Bernice and Otis were not in sight. He wandered back inside and found Otis in front of the women's dressing-room in the centre of a group of young men. Otis was talking excitedly.

'She's gone in to fix her hair,' he said wildly. 'Then I'll have to dance another hour with her.'

There was general laughter.

'Why don't some of you cut in and take her away from me?' Otis complained.

'Don't worry, Otis,' said Warren, smiling. 'I've come to give you a rest.'

A girl may be beautiful or brilliant, but if men do not cut in on her frequently at dances, she is in a difficult position. Young people in this **jazz**-loving **generation** are naturally restless. The idea of dancing more than one dance with the same girl is hateful to them. And if a young man is forced to dance a whole evening with a girl, she can be sure he will never ask her to dance again.

Warren danced the next full dance with Bernice, then he led her to a table outside. There was a moment's silence while she busily rearranged her dress.

'It's hotter here than in Eau Claire,' she said.

Warren yawned.

'Are you going to be here much longer?' he asked.

'Another week,' she answered.

Warren moved uncomfortably on his chair. Then suddenly he decided to try a different line of conversation. He turned and looked at her eyes.

'You've got an awfully kissable mouth,' he began quietly.

This was a remark he had used before at college parties. Bernice jumped and her face became red. No one had ever made a remark like that to her before.

'How dare you!' — the words had leapt out before she realized it, and she bit her lip. Although it was too late, she decided to be amused and gave Warren a smile.

Warren was annoyed. Girls didn't usually take that remark seriously. He changed the topic.

'Jim Strain and Ethel Demorest are here as usual,' he commented.

This was more like the sort of conversation Bernice was used to, but she felt a slight regret as the subject changed. Men did not talk to her about kissable mouths, but she knew that they talked like that to other girls.

'Oh, yes,' she said. 'I hear they've been going out together like this for years without a penny. Isn't it silly?'

Warren's disgust increased. Jim Strain was a close friend of his brother's. And anyway it was stupid to laugh at people because they didn't have any money. But Bernice had not intended to laugh at them, she was simply nervous.

2

When Marjorie and Bernice reached home at half past midnight, they said good night at the top of the stairs. Although they were cousins, they were not close friends. In fact, Marjorie had no close female friends – she considered girls stupid. Bernice, on the other hand, had hoped that she and Marjorie would share their secrets. She had looked forward to long talks full of girlish laughter and tears. For her these were an important part of all feminine conversation. However, she found Marjorie rather cold. For Bernice it was as difficult to talk to Marjorie as it was to talk to men. Marjorie never laughed in a girlish way, she was never frightened and rarely embarrassed; in fact, she had few of the qualities that Bernice considered truly feminine.

While Bernice was busy cleaning her teeth this night, she wondered for the hundredth time why she never had any attention when she was away from home. Her parents were rich and gave her every social advantage, but she never imagined that could be a reason. She did not realize that she would have danced the whole evening with one man if Marjorie had not used her powers of persuasion. But she knew that even in Eau Claire other girls with fewer social advantages and less physical attractiveness had more success than she did. She thought this must be because they did not have the same principles as she had. But it had never worried her. Her mother told her that girls like that cheapened themselves, and that men really respected girls like Bernice.

She turned out the light in her bathroom and decided to go in and chat for a while with her Aunt Josephine. She went down the hall towards her aunt's room. Hearing voices inside, she stopped near the partly opened door. Then she heard her own name. She did not intend to listen, but the conversation going on inside her aunt's room captured her attention.

'She's absolutely hopeless!' It was Marjorie's voice. 'Oh, I know what you're going to say! So many people have told you how pretty and sweet she is, and how she can cook! What of it? She doesn't enjoy herself. Men don't like her.'

'Bernice doesn't need cheap popularity.'

Mrs Harvey sounded annoyed.

'Popularity is everything when you're eighteen,' said Marjorie. 'I've done my best. I've been polite, and I've persuaded men to dance with her, but they don't like to be bored.'

'People have no manners these days.'

Mrs Harvey could not understand modern situations. When she was a girl, young ladies who belonged to nice families always enjoyed themselves.

'Well,' said Marjorie, 'I can't be there to support her all the time. These days every girl has to take care of herself. I've even tried to give her a few hints about clothes and things, and she's been angry every time. She knows she's not getting much attention, but she probably thinks she's a better person than me because of it. All unpopular girls think that way.'

'I know Bernice is not very lively,' interrupted Mrs Harvey, 'but you ought to be able to do something for her.'

Marjorie sighed.

'Not very lively! I've never heard her say anything to a boy except that it's hot, or that the dance-floor is crowded, or that she's going to school in New York next year. Sometimes she asks them what kind of car they have and tells them the kind she has. Thrilling!'

There was a short silence, and then Mrs Harvey repeated:

'But I know that other girls who are not so sweet or attractive get boyfriends. Martha Carey, for example, is fat and loud; and Roberta Dillon is so thin this year, but they both——'

'But mother,' interrupted Marjorie impatiently, 'Martha is cheerful and awfully amusing, and Roberta's a marvellous dancer. She's always been popular.'

Mrs Harvey yawned.

'I think it's that crazy Indian blood in Bernice,' continued Marjorie. 'Indian women all just sat around and never said anything.'

'Go to bed, you silly child,' laughed Mrs Harvey. 'When I told you that story about her mother's family, I didn't think you were going to remember it. And I think most of your ideas are perfectly idiotic,' she finished sleepily.

There was another silence while Marjorie wondered whether to continue. Deciding that it was pointless, she said good night. When she came out into the hall, it was quite empty.

While Marjorie was breakfasting late next day, Bernice came into the room with a rather stiff good morning. She sat down opposite and stared across at Marjorie.

'What's the matter?' enquired Marjorie, rather puzzled.

Bernice paused before she said anything.

'I heard what you said about me to your mother last night.'

Marjorie was alarmed, but her voice was calm when she spoke.

'Where were you?'

'In the hall. I didn't intend to listen – at first.'

Marjorie looked at her sharply, then dropped her eyes and became very interested in her breakfast.

'I suppose I'd better go back to Eau Claire – if I'm too much trouble for you.' Bernice's voice was shaking as she continued: 'I've tried to be nice, and – and now I've been insulted. I was never so unkind to a visitor.'

Marjorie was silent.

'But I see you don't want me here. Your friends don't like me.' Bernice paused, and then she remembered something Marjorie had said. 'Of course I was angry last week when you hinted that my dress was not suitable. Don't you think I know how to dress myself?'

'No,' said Marjorie quietly.

'What?'

'I didn't say anything,' said Marjorie. 'I said that it was better to wear the same dress for three parties in a row if it suits you than to wear three different, but unsuitable ones.'

'Do you think that was a very nice thing to say?'

'I wasn't trying to be nice.' Then, after a pause: 'When do you want to go?'

Bernice was shocked.

'Oh!' It was a little half-cry.

Marjorie looked up.

'Didn't you say you were going?'

'Yes, but——'

'Oh, you just wanted to see how I would react!'

They stared at each other across the breakfast table for a moment. Then Bernice burst into tears. Marjorie's eyes showed boredom.

'You're my cousin,' cried Bernice. 'I'm v–v–visiting you. I was supposed to stay a month, and if I go home my mother will know and she'll wah–wonder——'

Marjorie waited until the tears quietened.

'I'll give you some money,' she said coldly, 'and you can spend this last week where you want. There's a very nice hotel——'

Bernice stood up suddenly and ran from the room.

An hour later, while Marjorie was in the library writing a letter, Bernice reappeared, very red-eyed and consciously calm. She did not look at Marjorie, but took a book and sat down, as if to read. Marjorie continued writing. When the clock showed midday, Bernice closed her book noisily.

'I suppose I'd better get my train ticket.'

'Just wait till I finish this letter,' said Marjorie without looking round. 'I want to mail it today.'

Her pen scratched busily for another minute. Then she turned and sat back in her chair. Again Bernice had to speak first.

'Do you want me to go home?'

'Well,' said Marjorie, considering, 'I suppose if you're not having a good time, you'd better go.'

'Don't you think you could show more common kindness?'

15

'Oh, please don't talk like an old woman!' cried Marjorie impatiently. 'You seem to have got all your ideas from the sort of books that your mother read when she was a girl, books about perfect little women with empty heads.'

'They were good enough for our mothers.'

Marjorie laughed.

'Our mothers are all right, but they know very little about their daughters' problems.'

Bernice sat stiffly upright.

'Please don't talk about my mother.'

Marjorie laughed.

'I don't think I mentioned her.'

Bernice felt she had to get back to the topic.

'Do you think you've been fair with me?'

'I've done my best. You're a difficult one.'

Bernice's eyes reddened.

'I think you're hard and selfish, and you haven't a feminine quality in you.'

'Oh, no,' cried Marjorie in desperation. 'You little fool. Girls like you are responsible for all the boring, colourless marriages. Those silly weaknesses that people call "feminine qualities". What a pity when a man with imagination marries a girl and finds that, despite her pretty face and pretty clothes, she's just a helpless, complaining cowardly creature.'

Bernice's mouth had fallen half open.

'The womanly woman,' continued Marjorie. 'She spends her life criticizing girls like me who really do have a good time.'

Bernice's mouth opened wider as Marjorie's voice rose.

'If a girl is ugly, she has some excuse for complaining. But you're starting life without any disadvantages. If you expect me to cry with you, you'll be disappointed. Go or stay, just as you like.' And picking up her letters she left the room.

Bernice did not appear at lunch, saying she had a headache. She and Marjorie were supposed to go out together with a couple of boys that afternoon, but the headache continued and Marjorie went out alone. When she returned late in the afternoon, she found Bernice with a strangely fixed expression waiting for her in her bedroom.

'I've decided,' said Bernice, 'that maybe you're right about things. If you'll tell me why your friends aren't interested in me, I'll see if I can do what you want me to.'

Marjorie was at the mirror combing her hair.

'Are you serious?'

'Yes.'

'Without questions? Will you do exactly what I say?'

'Well, I—'

'Will you do exactly as I say?'

'If they're sensible things.'

'They're not. Sensible things won't help you.'

'Are you going to make suggestions – to recommend—'

'Yes, everything. If I tell you to do something, you'll have to do it. Write home and tell your mother you're going to stay for another two weeks.'

'If you'll tell me—'

'All right – I'll just give you a few examples now. First, you have no natural confidence. Why not? Because you're never sure about your personal appearance. When a girl knows that she looks right, she can forget that part of her. That's success. The more parts of you you can afford to forget, the more success you have.'

'Don't I look all right?'

'No – for example, you never take care of your eyebrows. They'd be beautiful if you took care of them. You're going to brush them so that they'll grow straight.'

Bernice lifted the brows in question.

'Do you mean to say that men notice eyebrows?'

'Yes – subconsciously. And when you go home, you ought to have your teeth straightened a little.'

'But I thought,' interrupted Bernice, 'that you hated little feminine things like that.'

'I hate silly feminine minds,' answered Marjorie. 'But a girl has to be feminine in person. If she looks like a million dollars, she can talk about Russia, football or the financial market, and people will listen.'

'What else?'

'Oh, I'm just beginning! There's your dancing.'

'Don't I dance all right?'

'No, you don't – you push a man while you're dancing, yes, you do – ever so slightly. I noticed it when we were dancing together yesterday.'

'Go on.' Bernice could hardly speak.

'Well, you've got to learn to be nice to men who are not successful with girls. You look as if you've been insulted whenever you have to dance with one of the less popular boys. A girl can't afford to be unkind to them. They're the big part of any crowd. You can practise your conversation very well with young boys who are too shy to talk. And boys who can't dance are the best dancing practice.'

Bernice gave a deep sigh, but Marjorie had not finished.

'If you go to a dance and really amuse three unpopular boys who dance with you, you've done something. They'll come back next time. Gradually the attractive boys will see that you're cut in on frequently. They'll realize there's no danger of getting stuck with you – then they'll dance with you.'

'Yes,' agreed Bernice weakly. 'I think I begin to see.'

'And finally,' concluded Marjorie, 'don't worry about the rest. The rest will just come. You'll wake up some morning knowing you've got it, and men will know it too.'

Bernice stood up.

'It's been awfully kind of you – but nobody's ever talked to me like this before, and I feel confused.'

Marjorie made no answer, but stared at herself in the mirror.

'It's good of you to help me,' continued Bernice.

Still Marjorie made no answer, and Bernice thought perhaps she seemed too grateful.

'I know you don't like fine feelings,' she said quietly.

Marjorie turned to her quickly.

'Oh, I wasn't thinking about that. I was wondering whether we should **bob** your hair.'

Bernice fell back onto the bed with a little scream.

4

On the following Wednesday evening there was a dinner-dance at the club. Bernice was slightly disappointed when she found she was sitting next to Charley Paulson. But she remembered Marjorie's instructions and turned to him.

'Do you think I ought to bob my hair, Mr Charley Paulson?'

Charley looked up in surprise.

'Why?'

'Because I'm considering it. It's such a sure and easy way of attracting attention.'

Charley smiled pleasantly. He could not know that Bernice had been practising this. He replied that he didn't know much about bobbed hair.

'I want to be a rebel, you see,' said Bernice, and she informed him that short hair was an important first step. She added that she wanted to ask his advice because he was so critical about girls.

Charley was pleased.

'So I've decided,' Bernice continued, raising her voice slightly, 'that early next week I'm going down to the **barber**-shop at the Sevier Hotel. I'll sit in the first chair and get my hair bobbed.'

She hesitated, noticing that the people near her had paused in their conversation and were listening. But after a second she finished her speech. 'Of course, you'll have to pay for tickets if you want to come and watch. If you all come down and encourage me, I'll make sure you get good seats.'

There was general laughter, and G. Reece Stoddard turned to her quickly and said in a low voice: 'I'll take a seat in the first row straight away.'

She smiled at him as if he had said something particularly brilliant.

'Do you believe in bobbed hair?' asked G. Reece in the same low voice.

'I think it's shameful,' said Bernice slowly. 'But, of course, you've either got to amuse people or feed them or shock them.' Bernice had learnt this line from Marjorie, who had borrowed it from Oscar Wilde. The men laughed, and the girls gave a series of quick silent looks. Then Bernice turned again to Charley.

'I want to ask you your opinion of several people. I imagine that you're a wonderful judge of character.'

Charley was thrilled.

Two hours later, Warren MacIntyre was standing by himself at the side of the dance-floor. Marjorie had disappeared and he was trying to guess where to and who with. He was watching the dancers without paying much attention. But then he began to notice something unusual. Bernice, Marjorie's cousin, had been cut in on several times in the past five minutes. A moment ago she had been dancing with a visiting boy. Now she was dancing with G. Reece Stoddard himself. And there was Charley Paulson, coming across the floor towards her with an enthusiastic determination in his eye.

The next time Bernice danced near him, Warren looked at her carefully. Yes, she was pretty, definitely pretty, and tonight her face was lively and excited. She looked as if she was enjoying herself. He liked the way she had arranged her hair, and that was a very attractive dress. But what a pity she was so dull!

His thoughts went back to Marjorie. He was sure that her disappearance this evening would be like other disappearances. When she reappeared, he would demand to know where she had been, and she would refuse to tell him. What a pity she was so sure of him! She was confident that no other girl in town interested him.

Warren sighed. It seemed impossible to win Marjorie's affection. He looked up. Bernice was again dancing with the visiting boy. Half unconsciously, Warren started to move in her direction. He hesitated, then told himself that he only wanted to be kind to the poor girl. He walked towards her – and immediately knocked into G. Reece Stoddard.

'Pardon me,' said Warren.

But G. Reece had not stopped to apologize. He had again cut in on Bernice.

◆   ◆   ◆   ◆

That night at one o'clock, before saying good night, Marjorie took a last look at Bernice's shining eyes.

'So it worked?'

'Oh, Marjorie, yes!' cried Bernice.

'I saw you were having a good time.'

'I was!'

'Well, we'll arrange something new tomorrow. Good night.'

'Good night.'

As Bernice was brushing her hair, she thought back over the evening's events. She had followed instructions exactly. Even when Charley Paulson had cut in for the eighth time, she had pretended to be delighted. She had not talked about the weather or Eau Claire or cars or her school. But a few minutes before she fell asleep a rebellious thought came into her mind. Of course Marjorie had helped. But it was she, Bernice, who had done it. Her voice had said the words, her lips had smiled, her feet had danced. Marjorie, nice girl – proud, though – nice evening – nice boys – like Warren – Warren – what's his name – Warren.

She fell asleep.

5

For Bernice the next week was a week of discovery. Knowing that people really enjoyed looking at her and listening to her, she began to feel more self-confident. Of course there were mistakes at first, but many more successes. Little Otis Ormonde followed her around like a pet dog, and G. Reece Stoddard made several afternoon visits.

Perhaps the best-known and most successful line in Bernice's conversation was the one about the bobbing of her hair.

'Oh, Bernice, when are you going to get your hair bobbed?'

'The day after tomorrow maybe,' she replied laughing. 'Will you come and see me? Because I'm relying on you, you know.'

'Will we? You know! But you'd better hurry up.'

Bernice laughed. She had no intention of doing anything to her hair.

'Soon. You'd be surprised.'

But probably her most important success was the attention she received from Warren MacIntyre. His grey car was parked in front of the Harveys' house daily. Soon everyone knew that Marjorie's most loyal admirer was now showing more interest in Marjorie's guest. How long would Marjorie put up with it? That was the question of the moment. Warren called Bernice on the phone twice a day, sent her notes, and they were frequently seen together in his car. When anybody joked to Marjorie about it, she only laughed. She said she was glad that Warren had at last found someone who valued him.

One afternoon, three days before the end of her visit, Bernice was waiting in the hall for Warren. They were going to a party and Bernice was in a happy mood. Marjorie was also going to a party, and when she appeared, Bernice was unprepared for an argument. Marjorie did her work in three sentences.

'You'd better forget Warren,' she said coldly.

'What?' Bernice was amazed.

'You'd better stop making a fool of yourself over Warren MacIntyre. He's not interested in you.'

For a moment they both stared at each other. Then the two cars arrived and they both hurried out.

All through the party Bernice tried to master a growing sense of fear. She had offended Marjorie. With the most innocent intentions in the world she had stolen what belonged to Marjorie. She felt suddenly and horribly guilty. Later in the evening, when they were sitting in a circle, the storm gradually broke. Little Otis Ormonde started it without realizing.

'When are you going back to school, Otis,' someone had asked.

'Me? On the day Bernice gets her hair bobbed.'

'Then your education's over,' said Marjorie quickly. 'She's only pretending. She's not going to do it. Hadn't you realized?'

'Is that true?' demanded Otis, turning to Bernice.

Bernice's ears burned as she tried to think up a suitable reply. But her imagination failed her.

'You shouldn't believe everything people tell you, you know, Otis,' said Marjorie pleasantly.

'Well,' said Otis, 'maybe you're right, but Bernice——'

'Was that really all a joke?' interrupted Roberta curiously.

Bernice hesitated. She knew that she was expected to say something clever, but she felt her cousin's cold stare, and she froze.

'I don't know.'

'Nonsense!' said Marjorie. 'Admit it!'

Bernice saw that Warren's eyes were fixed on her questioningly.

'Oh, I don't know,' she repeated steadily. Her cheeks were red.

'Nonsense!' remarked Marjorie again.

'Come on, Bernice,' said Otis. 'Tell her she's wrong.'

Bernice looked round again – it seemed impossible to escape Warren's eyes.

'I like bobbed hair,' she said in a hurry, 'and I intend to bob mine.'

'When?' demanded Marjorie.

'Any time.'

'Why not now?' suggested Roberta.

Otis jumped to his feet.

'Great!' he cried. 'We'll have a summer bobbing party. Sevier Hotel barber-shop, I think you said.'

Immediately everyone was standing up. Bernice's heart knocked violently.

'What?' she began.

Marjorie's voice rose above the general noise, very clear and hard.

'Don't worry – she won't do it.'

'Come on, Bernice!' cried Otis, starting towards the door.

Four eyes – Warren's and Marjorie's – stared at her, demanding whether she dared. For another second she hesitated wildly.

'All right,' she said suddenly, 'I think I will.'

The journey into town beside Warren, followed by the others in Roberta's car, took a few minutes, but it seemed an hour. Bernice felt like a criminal on the way to the electric chair. She wanted to cry out that it was all a mistake. But nothing could help her now.

Warren was silent, and when they came to the hotel, he nodded to Bernice, who was the first to get out of the car. A laughing crowd emptied out of Roberta's car into the street and into the shop.

Bernice stood outside and looked at the sign – Sevier barber-shop. The first barber, dressed in a white coat, stood waiting by the first chair, smoking a cigarette. He must have known she was coming; he must have been waiting all week. Would they tie a scarf round her eyes?

'All right, Bernice,' said Warren quickly.

With her chin in the air she crossed the pavement, pushed open the door and went up to the first barber without even looking at the noisy crowd sitting on the waiting seats.

'I want you to bob my hair.'

The first barber's mouth slid half open. His cigarette dropped to the floor.

'Huh?'

Bernice stood outside and looked at the sign. The barber, dressed in a white coat, stood waiting by a chair, smoking a cigarette.

'My hair – bob it!'

Without further delay, Bernice sat in the chair. A man in the chair next to her turned and stared, his face covered in shaving cream. One barber lost his concentration and spoiled little Willy Schuneman's monthly haircut. Mr O'Reilly in the last chair swore as a razor cut into his cheek.

Outside people stopped and stared; half a dozen small boys pressed their faces against the window.

But Bernice saw nothing, heard nothing. She was only conscious of the fact that this man in the white coat had removed first one comb then another. She felt his fingers pulling at hairpins. And she knew that this hair, this wonderful hair of hers, was going. She would never again feel its weight as it hung down her back. For a second she was close to tears. Then she saw Marjorie's mouth curling in a smile, as if to say:

'Give up and get down from that chair! You tried to cheat me and I put you to the test. You see you haven't got a chance.'

And Bernice gripped the sides of the chair. Her eyes narrowed and her face took on a curious fixed expression that Marjorie remembered long afterwards.

Twenty minutes later the barber turned the chair to face the mirror. Bernice was afraid to look at the damage that had been done. Her hair was not curly, and now it lay lifeless and flat, either side of her suddenly pale face. It was ugly – she had known it would be ugly. Her face's chief beauty had been a classical simplicity. Now that was gone and she was – well, ordinary, like a librarian who had left her glasses at home.

As she climbed down from the chair she tried to smile and failed. She saw two of the girls look at one another quickly. She noticed Marjorie's mouth curved in a smile. And she saw that Warren's eyes were suddenly very cold.

There was a painful silence, then she spoke.

'You see, I've done it.'

'Yes, you've – done it,' admitted Warren.

'Do you like it?'

There was a slow 'Sure' from two or three voices, followed by another pause. Then Marjorie turned to Warren.

'Would you drive me to the cleaners?' she asked. 'I've got to fetch a dress there before supper. Roberta's driving straight home and she can take the others.'

Warren stared absently out of the window. Then for a moment his eyes rested coldly on Bernice before they turned to Marjorie.

'I'd be glad to,' he said slowly.

6

Bernice did not fully realize the cruel trap that had been laid for her until she met her aunt just before dinner.

'Why, Bernice!'

'I've bobbed it, Aunt Josephine.'

'Why, child!'

'Do you like it?'

'Why, Bernice!'

'I suppose I've shocked you.'

'No, but what will Mrs Deyo think tomorrow night? Bernice, why didn't you wait until after the Deyo's dance?'

'It was sudden, Aunt Josephine. Anyway, why does it matter to Mrs Deyo particularly?'

'Why, child,' cried Mrs Harvey, 'she hates bobbed hair. She gave a talk at the last meeting of the Thursday Club about the "The Foolish Ideas of the Younger Generation" and she spent fifteen minutes speaking about bobbed hair. And the dance is for you and Marjorie!'

'I'm sorry.'

'Oh, Bernice, what'll your mother say? She'll think I let you do it.'

'I'm sorry.'

Bernice stayed in her room all evening. When she had undressed for the night, the door opened and Marjorie came in.

'Bernice,' she said, 'I'm awfully sorry about the Deyo dance. Honestly, I'd forgotten all about it.'

'It's all right,' said Bernice shortly. Standing in front of the mirror, she passed her comb slowly through her short hair.

'I'll take you into town tomorrow,' continued Marjorie, 'and the hairdresser will fix it so you'll look fine. I didn't imagine you'd do it. I'm really very sorry.'

'Oh, it's all right.'

Then Bernice watched as Marjorie shook her own hair over her shoulder and began to twist it into two long, blond **braids**, until she looked like a German princess. Bernice thought of the things people would say tomorrow. She could see their faces. Perhaps Mrs Deyo would hear the news and send round an icy little note asking her not to come. And behind her back they would all laugh and know that Marjorie had made a fool of her. Her one chance of success had been spoiled by a jealous, selfish girl. She sat down suddenly in front of the mirror.

'I like it,' she said, biting her lip. 'I think it will suit me.'

Marjorie smiled.

'It looks all right. Don't worry.'

'I won't.'

'Good night, Bernice.'

But as the door closed, Bernice made a sudden decision. She leapt to her feet and dragged her travelling bag out from underneath the bed. It was rapidly filled with all that she would need for the journey. Then she turned to her trunk. In three-quarters of an hour it was packed. She sat down at her desk and wrote a short note to Mrs Harvey, explaining her reasons for going. She addressed it and laid it on her pillow. She looked quickly at her watch. The train left at one. She knew that if she walked to the Marlborough Hotel she could easily get a taxi.

Suddenly she took a sharp breath and an odd expression came into her eyes. It was like the fixed look she had had in the barber's chair – in some way a development of it. It was quite a new look for Bernice – and it meant something.

She went softly to the desk and picked something out of a drawer. Then she turned out all the lights and stood quietly until she could see in the darkness. Gently she pushed open the door to Marjorie's room. Marjorie was sleeping.

She was by the side of Marjorie's bed now, very purposeful and calm. She acted fast. Bending over, she took one of the braids of Marjorie's hair. She found the point nearest the head, then reached down with the scissors and cut it. She held her breath. Marjorie had moved in her sleep. Bernice cut off the other braid, paused for a moment and then ran silently back to her own room.

Downstairs she opened the big front door, closed it carefully behind her and set off in the moonlight. She felt strangely excited and happy. After she had been walking for a minute, she discovered that she was still holding the two blonde braids. She laughed unexpectedly and had to shut her mouth hard. She was passing Warren's house now. Without thinking, she put down her bag and threw the braids like pieces of rope at the front door. They landed with a dull sound. She laughed again, loudly.

'Huh!' she shouted wildly. '**Scalp** the selfish thing!'

Then, picking up her bag, she set off at a half-run down the moonlit street.

Bending over, she took one of the braids of Marjorie's hair and cut it with the scissors.

When John Andros felt old, he comforted himself with the thought that life would continue through his child. His fears were calmed when he heard his child's quick footsteps or the sound of his child's voice talking nonsense to him over the telephone. His wife called him at the office every afternoon at three, and he looked forward to these conversations as one of the colourful minutes of his day.

He was not physically old, but his life had been a series of struggles up a series of hills. At thirty-eight, having won his battles against ill-health and poverty, he had few dreams left. Even his feelings about his little girl had limits. She had come between him and his wife, and it was for the child's sake that they had moved to a small town in the country. They paid for fresh country air with endless servant troubles and the daily journeys to and from work by train.

Little Ede interested him chiefly as an example of a young life. He liked to take her on his knees and examine the soft hairs on her scalp and her eyes of morning blue. But after ten minutes the endless curiosity of the child began to test his patience. He easily lost his temper and got annoyed when things were broken. One Sunday afternoon when she had spoiled a game of cards, he had been so angry that his wife had burst into tears. This was foolish and John was ashamed of himself. Such things could not be avoided. It was impossible that little Ede should spend all day in the baby room upstairs. Her mother frequently reminded him that she was becoming more nearly a 'real person' every day.

She was two and a half, and this afternoon, for example, she was going to a baby party. Edith, her mother, had telephoned this information to the office. Little Ede had repeated it, shouting, 'I yam going to a *pantry*!' into John's unsuspecting left ear.

'Call round at the Markeys' when you get home, won't you, dear?' said her mother. 'It'll be funny. Ede's going to be all dressed up in her new pink dress——'

The conversation ended suddenly with a tiny scream. It sounded as if the telephone had been pulled violently to the floor. John laughed and decided to catch an early train home. The idea of a baby party in someone else's house amused him.

'What a wonderful mess!' he thought, smiling to himself. 'A dozen mothers, and each one looking only at her own child. All the babies breaking things and grabbing at the cake. And each mama going home thinking her own child was so much better than every other child there.'

He was in a good mood today – all the things in his life were going better than they had ever gone before. When he got off the train at his station, he shook his head at a taxi man and began to walk up the long hill towards his house through the cold December evening. It was only six o'clock, but the moon was out and shining with proud brilliance on the thin sugary snow that lay over the gardens.

As he walked along, taking deep breaths of cold air, he began to wonder how Ede compared to other children of her own age. He wondered if she would look more grown up in her new pink dress. He walked faster and passed his own house. The party was at the Markeys' next door.

As he climbed the steps and rang the bell, he heard voices inside, and he was glad he was not too late. Then he lifted his head and listened – the voices were not children's voices, but they were loud and angry. There were at least three different voices. One of them rose to a sharp cry and he recognized it immediately as his wife's.

'There's been some trouble,' he thought quickly.

He tried the door, found it unlocked and pushed it open.

♦   ♦   ♦   ♦

The baby party started at half past four, but Edith waited. She guessed that the new dress would have a more sensational effect if it was seen beside other costumes which were not as fresh and clean. So she planned the arrival of little Ede and herself for five o'clock. When they arrived, the party was already lively. Four baby girls and nine baby boys were dancing to the music of a record.

As Edith and her daughter entered, there was a cry of 'How sweet!' It was directed towards little Ede, who stood looking around shyly and fingering the edges of her pink dress. She was passed along a row of mamas, each one of whom said 'swe—e—et!' to her and held her pink little hand before passing her on to the next. After some encouragement and a few gentle pushes she joined the dance and became an active member of the party.

Edith stood near the door talking to Mrs Markey. She did not like Mrs Markey. She considered her both sharp-tongued and common. But John and Joe Markey were friendly and went in to work together on the train every morning, so the two women pretended to be good neighbours. They were always saying that it was a pity they never visited one another. And they were always planning the kind of parties that began with 'You'll have to come to dinner with us soon', but never developed any further.

'Little Ede looks a perfect darling,' said Mrs Markey, smiling and wetting her lips in a way that particularly annoyed Edith. 'So *grown up* – I can't *believe* it!'

Edith wondered if Mrs Markey referred to Ede as 'little Ede' because Billy Markey weighed almost five pound more, although he was several months younger. She accepted a cup of tea and sat down with two other ladies on a sofa. She immediately started on the real business of the afternoon, which consisted of describing the recent progress of her child.

An hour passed. The children became bored with dancing and ran into the dining room. From there they made an attack on the door to the kitchen and were rescued by an army of mothers. They immediately set off again and ran back to the dining room and the kitchen door. The word 'over-excited' was used and small white faces were dried with small white handkerchiefs. There was a general attempt to make the babies sit down, but the babies jumped off their mothers' knees with loud cries of 'Down! Down!' And the rush into the dining room began again.

This game ended when the food and drink were brought in, including a large cake and saucers of ice cream. Billy Markey, a solid laughing baby with red hair and thick legs, took the first piece of cake. Drinks were poured and the children ate, greedily but without confusion. They had behaved remarkably well all afternoon. They were modern babies who ate and slept at regular hours, so their tempers and their faces were healthy and pink. Thirty years ago parties were not so peaceful.

After the food and drink the visitors began to leave. Edith looked at her watch. It was almost six and John had not arrived. She wanted him to see Ede with the other children. She wanted him to see how calm and polite and intelligent she was.

'You're a darling,' she whispered to her child, holding her closely. 'Do you know you're a darling? Do you *know* you're a darling?'

Ede laughed. '**Bow-wow**,' she said suddenly.

'Bow-wow?' Edith looked around. She could not see a dog, a 'bow-wow', anywhere. 'There isn't any bow-wow,' she said.

'Bow-wow', repeated Ede. 'I want a bow-wow.'

Ede was pointing at Billy Markey who was holding his birthday present, a toy **bear**, in his arms.

'That isn't a bow-wow, dearest; that's a teddy-bear.'

'Teddy-bear?'

'Yes, that's a teddy-bear, and it belongs to Billy Markey. You don't want Billy Markey's teddy-bear, do you?'

Ede did want it.

She escaped from her mother and approached Billy Markey. Ede stood looking at him with a steady stare, and Billy laughed.

Edith looked at her watch again, this time impatiently. The party was smaller now. Besides Ede and Billy there were only two other babies. Why hadn't John come? It was selfish of him to be so late. He had no interest in the child. Other fathers had come to fetch their wives and they had stayed for a while and watched the party.

There was a sudden cry. Ede had pulled Billy's teddy-bear from his arms and when Billy had tried to take it back, she had simply pushed him to the floor.

'Why, Ede!' Edith was tempted to laugh.

Joe Markey, a handsome, broad-shouldered man of thirty-five, picked up his son and put him back on his feet. 'You're a fine fellow,' he said laughing. 'You let a girl push you over! You're a fine fellow.'

'Did he knock his head?' Mrs Markey asked quickly.

'No—o—o—o,' said Markey.

Billy had already forgotten the knock and was making an attempt to get his teddy-bear back. He grabbed a leg of the bear and pulled at it, but without success.

'No,' said Ede firmly.

Suddenly, encouraged by her earlier success, Ede dropped the teddy-bear, put her hands on Billy's shoulders and pushed him backwards off his feet. This time he landed less harmlessly. His head hit the floor with a dull hollow sound. He took a breath and let out a scream.

There was a sudden cry. Ede had pulled Billy's teddy-bear from his arms.

Immediately the room was in confusion. Markey hurried to his son, but his wife reached the injured baby before him. She took him in her arms.

'Oh, *Billy*,' she cried, 'What a terrible knock! She deserves a slap.'

Edith had rushed immediately to her daughter. She heard this remark and her lips came together sharply.

'Why, Ede,' she whispered, 'you bad girl!'

Ede put back her little head suddenly and laughed. It was a loud laugh, with a sound of victory. Unfortunately it was also an infectious laugh. Before her mother realized that it was a **sensitive** situation, she too had laughed. Edith's laugh was like her daughter's, with the same sound.

Then she stopped.

Mrs Markey's face had turned red with anger. Joe Markey was feeling the back of his son's head with one finger. He looked at her quickly.

'It's a bad knock,' he said. 'I'll get some cream to put on it.'

But Mrs Markey had lost her temper. 'I don't see anything funny about a child being hurt,' she said in a shaking voice.

Little Ede had been looking at her mother curiously. She had noticed that her own laugh had caused her mother's laugh, and she wondered if the same cause would always have the same effect. So she chose this moment to throw back her head and laugh again.

For her mother this was too much. Pressing her handkerchief to her mouth, she laughed uncontrollably. It was more than nervousness. She felt that in an odd way she was laughing with her child. They were laughing together. It was those two against the world.

While Markey rushed upstairs to the bathroom for the cream, his wife was walking up and down, holding the screaming boy in her arms.

'Please go home!' she burst out suddenly. 'The child is badly hurt, and if you won't be quiet, you'd better go home.'

'Very well,' said Edith, losing her temper. 'I've never seen such a lot of trouble about nothing——'

'Get out!' cried Mrs Markey. 'There's the door, get out – I never want to see you in our house again. You or your horrible spoilt little child either.'

Edith had taken her daughter's hand and was moving quickly towards the door. But hearing this remark, she stopped and turned around.

'Don't you dare talk about my child like that!'

Mrs Markey did not answer but continued walking up and down, talking to herself and to Billy in a low voice.

Edith began to cry.

'I will get out,' she said. 'I've never heard anybody so rude and common in my life. I'm glad your baby was pushed down – he's nothing but a f–fat little fool anyway.'

Joe Markey reached the bottom of the stairs just in time to hear this remark.

'Why, Mrs Andros,' he said sharply, 'can't you see the child is hurt. You really ought to control yourself.'

'C–control myself!' said Edith in a broken voice. 'You'd better ask her to c–control herself. I've never heard anybody so c–common in my life.'

'She's insulting me!' Mrs Markey was now red with anger. 'Did you hear what she said, Joe? Please put her out of the house. If she won't go, just take her by the shoulders and put her out!'

'Don't you dare touch me!' cried Edith. 'I'm going just as soon as I can find my coat!'

Blind with tears, she took a step towards the hall. It was just at this moment that the door opened and John Andros walked in.

'John!' cried Edith, and ran to him wildly.

'What's the matter? Why, what's the matter?'

'They're – they're putting me out!' she cried. 'He'd just started to take me by the shoulders and put me out. I want my coat!'

'That's not true,' said Markey hurriedly. 'Nobody's going to put you out.' He turned to John. 'Nobody's going to put her out,' he repeated. 'She's——'

'What do you mean "put her out"?' demanded John. 'What's all this talk anyway?'

'Oh, let's go!' cried Edith. 'I want to go. They're so *common*, John!'

'Look here!' Markey's face darkened. 'You've said that often enough. You're acting crazy.'

'They called Ede "spoilt".'

For the second time that afternoon little Ede expressed emotion at an unsuitable moment. Confused and frightened at the shouting voices, she began to cry. And her tears seemed to say that she felt the insult in her heart.

'What's the idea of this?' John began. 'Do you insult your guests in your own house?'

'It's your wife who's been insulting people,' replied Markey angrily. 'In fact, your baby started all the trouble.'

John gave a short laugh. 'Are you accusing a little baby?' he enquired. 'That's a fine manly business!'

'Don't talk to him, John,' insisted Edith. 'Find my coat!'

'You must be a poor fellow,' went on John angrily, 'if you exercise your temper on a helpless baby.'

'I've never heard anything so twisted in my life,' shouted Markey. 'If your wife would shut her mouth for a minute——'

'Wait a minute! You're not talking to a woman and child now——'

'Your wife comes in here and begins shouting about how common we are!' burst out Markey violently. 'Well, if we're so common, you'd better stay away! And you'd better get out now!'

Again John gave a short laugh.

'You're not only common,' he replied, 'you're obviously an awful coward.' He reached for the door handle. 'Come on, Edith.'

His wife took her daughter in her arms and stepped outside. Still looking at Markey, John started to follow.

'Wait a minute!' Markey took a step forward. He was shaking slightly and his eyes were red. 'Do you think you can say that and just walk out of here? Do you?'

Without a word John walked out of the door, leaving it open.

Edith had started to walk back home. After watching her until she reached her own front door, John turned back towards the open door. Markey was slowly coming down the steps. He took off his coat and threw it onto the snow beside the path. Then, sliding a little on the icy surface, he took a step forward.

At the first blow they both slipped and fell heavily to the ground. They rose and again pulled each other down. It was easier to stand in the thin snow beside the path. They rushed at each other, both hitting wildly.

The street was empty. They fought in silence except for their tired breaths and the dull sound as one or the other slipped and fell in the muddy snow. They could see each other clearly in the moonlight. Several times they both slipped down together. And then they twisted around wildly in the mud for a while.

For ten, twenty minutes they fought there senselessly in the moonlight. Their shirts were torn, and both were cut and

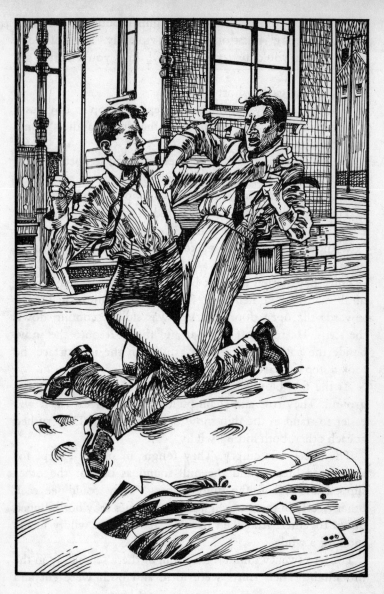

With a single blow they both fell to their hands and knees.

bleeding. They were so exhausted that they could stand only when they supported each other. With a single blow they both fell to their hands and knees.

But it was not exhaustion that ended the business. In fact, the meaninglessness of the fight was a reason for continuing. They stopped because they heard a man's footsteps coming along the pavement. They were lying on the ground in the shadow. When they heard these footsteps, they stopped fighting, stopped moving, stopped breathing. They lay close together like two boys playing a game until the footsteps had passed. Then, getting up, they looked at each other like two drunken men.

'I'm not going on with this thing anymore,' cried Markey.

'Nor am I,' said John Andros. 'I've had enough of this thing.'

Again they looked at each other, as if each one suspected the other of trying to restart the fight. Markey touched his lip, which was cut and bleeding. Then he swore softly, picked up his coat and shook the snow off it.

'Do you want to come in and get cleaned up?' he asked suddenly.

'No, thanks,' said John. 'I ought to be going home – my wife will be worried.'

He too picked up his coat.

'Well – good night,' he said hesitantly.

Suddenly they walked towards each other and shook hands. It was a firm handshake; John Andros put his arm around Markey's shoulder.

'No harm done,' he said in a broken voice.

'No – you?'

'No, no harm done.'

'Well,' said John Andros after a minute. 'I'll say good night.'

Dragging one leg slightly and with his coat over his arm, John Andros turned away.

The moonlight was still bright. Down at the station half a mile away he could hear the sound of the seven o'clock train.

◆   ◆   ◆   ◆

'But you must have been crazy,' cried Edith brokenly. 'I thought you were going to explain everything, fix it up and shake hands. That's why I went away.'

'Did you want us to fix it up?'

'Of course not; I never want to see them again. But I thought of course that was what you were going to do.' She was touching the cuts on his neck and back as he sat calmly in a hot bath. 'I'm going to get a doctor,' she insisted.

He shook his head. 'No, you aren't,' he answered. 'I don't want everyone in the town to hear about this.'

'I still don't understand how it all happened.'

'Neither do I,' he said. 'I suppose these baby parties can be quite rough.'

'Well, there's one good thing,' suggested Edith hopefully. 'I'm certainly glad we have beef steak in the house for tomorrow's dinner.'

'Why?'

'For your eye, of course. Do you know I very nearly ordered pork? Wasn't that the luckiest thing?'

Half an hour later John was dressed except for his collar, which was now too small for his neck. He tested the movements of his arms and legs in front of the mirror. 'I think I'll get myself fit and in better shape,' he said thoughtfully. 'I must be getting old.'

'You mean so next time you can beat him?'

'I did beat him,' he replied quickly. 'At least I beat him as much as he beat me. And there isn't going to be any next time. Don't you start calling people common any more. If you get in any trouble, you just take your coat and go home. Understand?'

'Yes dear,' she said quietly. 'I was very foolish and now I understand.'

He went out into the hall and paused by the baby's door.

'Is she asleep?'

'Yes. But you can go in and have a look at her – just to say good night.'

They went softly into the room and bent together over the bed. Little Ede was sleeping calmly. Her cheeks were pink with health and her little hands were tightly joined. John reached down and passed his hand lightly over the soft hair.

'She's asleep,' he said in a puzzled way.

'Naturally, after such an afternoon.'

'Miz Andros!' The servant's loud whisper floated into the room from the hall outside. 'Mr and Miz Markey are downstairs an' want to see you. Mr Markey, he's all cut up in pieces. His face looks like roast beef. An' Miz Markey, she's angry.'

'Why, how dare they?' cried Edith. 'Just tell them we're not home. I wouldn't go down for anything in the world.'

'You most certainly will.' John's voice was firm and hard.

'What?'

'You'll go down right now, and, whatever that other woman does, you'll apologize for what you said this afternoon. After that you don't have to see her again.'

'Why, John, I can't.'

'You've got to. And just remember that she probably hated to come over here twice as much as you hate to go downstairs.'

'Aren't you coming? Do I have to go alone?'

'I'll be down – in just a minute.'

John Andros waited until she closed the door behind her. Then he reached into the bed and picked up his daughter

45

wrapped in her blankets. He sat down in the chair, holding her tightly in his arms. She moved a little, and he held his breath, but she was sleeping deeply. In a moment she was resting in the hollow of his elbow. Slowly he bent his head until his cheek was against her bright hair. 'Dear little girl,' he whispered. 'Dear little girl, dear little girl.'

John Andros knew at last what he had fought for so wildly that evening. He had it now, he would keep it for ever, and for some time he sat there in the darkness with his daughter in his arms.

A SHORT TRIP HOME

1

I was near her. I had waited behind in order to share with her the short walk from the living-room to the front door. For me that was a lot. She had flowered suddenly and I, being a man and only a year older, hadn't flowered at all. She had the sure, clear confidence that comes to attractive American girls at about eighteen. There was magic suddenly in the soft hairs at the back of her neck.

She was already moving away from me into another world – the world of Joe Jelke and Jim Cathcart, who were waiting for us now in the car outside. In another year she would pass out of my sight for ever.

As I waited, I was conscious of the others outside in the snowy night. I felt the excitement of Christmas week and the excitement of Ellen here, filling the room with a special electricity. A servant came in from the dining-room, spoke to Ellen quietly and handed her a note. Ellen read it and her eyes lost their brilliance. Then she gave me an odd, distant look;

she probably didn't even see me. And without a word she followed the servant into the dining-room. I sat turning over the pages of a magazine for a quarter of an hour.

Joe Jelke came in, red-faced from the cold. He was a third year student at New Haven; I was in my first year. He was an important member of various clubs, and I admired and respected him.

'Isn't Ellen coming?'

'I don't know,' I answered. 'She was all ready.'

'Ellen!' he called. 'Ellen!'

He had left the front door open behind him and freezing air blew in from outside. He went halfway up the stairs and called again until Mrs Baker came and said that Ellen was downstairs. Then the servant appeared in the dining-room door. She seemed a little excited.

'Mr Jelke,' she called in a low voice.

Joe's face showed disappointment as he turned towards her. He sensed bad news.

'Miss Ellen says, you go to the party without her. She'll come later.'

He hesitated, confused. It was the last big dance before we all had to go back to college, and he was madly in love with Ellen. He wasn't the only one – there were three or four other young men with the same feelings towards Ellen. But he was rich and popular, and at the moment the most admired boy of St Paul. To me it seemed impossible that she could prefer another, but according to rumour she'd described Joe as much too perfect. I suppose he didn't have any mystery for her. And when a man is faced with a girl who isn't thinking of the practical side of marriage yet – well——

'She's in the kitchen,' said Joe angrily.'

'No, she's not.' The servant was a little afraid.

'She is.'

47

'She went out through the back door, Mr Jelke.'

'I'm going to see.'

I followed him. The Swedish servants washing dishes looked up as we came in. The back door was open and, as we walked outside, we saw the lights of a car turn the corner at the end of the back alley.

'I'm going after her,' Joe said slowly. 'I don't understand this at all.'

I was too surprised to argue. We hurried to his car and drove all over the district, looking into every car we saw. It was half an hour before Joe realized that the search was useless – St Paul is a city of almost three hundred thousand people. And Jim Cathcart reminded him that we had to pick up another girl too. Like a wounded animal, he sank into a corner.

Jim's girl was ready and impatient, but after what had happened her impatience didn't seem important. Joe Jelke was polite to her, but his conversation consisted of one burst of short, loud laughter. We drove to the hotel.

The driver approached the hotel on the wrong side. Because of that we suddenly saw Ellen Baker getting out of a small car. Even before we stopped, Joe Jelke had jumped excitedly from the car.

Ellen turned towards us. Her face had an absent look – a look of surprise, perhaps, but certainly not of alarm. In fact, she hardly seemed to see us. Joe approached her with an injured expression. I followed.

Seated in the small car was a hard, thin-faced man of about thirty-five. He had a scarred face and an unpleasant dark smile. His eyes were a sort of insult to the whole human family. They were the eyes of an animal, sleepy and quiet, observing the approach of a different kind of creature. They were helpless but fierce, unhopeful but confident. It was as if they knew that they were powerless to do anything, but

Seated in the small car was a hard, thin-faced man with a scarred face and an unpleasant smile.

extremely capable of profiting from a single sign of weakness in another.

In a curious way I recognized him. He was one of the sort of men I had seen standing around on street corners, in bars, garages, barber-shops and the entrances of theatres, watching through narrow eyes the people who hurried past. I had been conscious of this threatening type since I was a young boy and had always nervously avoided the half-lit borderland where he stood, watching and laughing at me. Once, in a dream, he had taken a few steps towards me and moved his head, saying, 'Hey, boy,' and I had run for the door in terror. This was that sort of man.

Joe and Ellen faced each other silently. She seemed only half awake. Suddenly the man in the car laughed. It was a noiseless laugh, almost nothing more than a shake of the head, but it was a definite insult. Joe had a quick temper, and I was not surprised when he turned to the man angrily and said:

'What's your trouble?'

The man waited a moment, his eyes staring. Then he laughed again in the same way. Ellen moved restlessly.

'Who is this – this –' Joe's voice shook with annoyance.

'Look out now,' said the man slowly.

Joe turned to me.

'Eddie, take Ellen and Catherine in, will you?' he said quickly.

'Look out now,' the man repeated.

Ellen made a little impatient sound with her tongue, but she followed me when I took her arm and moved towards the side door of the hotel. I thought it was strange that she should be so helpless. She seemed to accept the fact that trouble was about to start.

'Forget it, Joe!' I called back over my shoulder. 'Come inside!'

Ellen pulled my arm and we hurried on. As we went inside, I had the impression that the man was getting out of his car.

Ten minutes later I was waiting for the girls outside the women's dressing room when Joe Jelke and Jim Cathcart stepped out of the lift. Joe was very white and his eyes were heavy. There was blood over his left eye and on his white scarf.

'He hit Joe with **brass knuckles**,' Jim said in a low voice. 'Joe was unconscious for a minute or so. Go and ask for a bandage, will you?'

It was late and the hall was empty. The sounds of the dance came up from the floor below. When Ellen came out, I took her to a quiet room downstairs and told her what had happened.

'It was Joe's own fault,' she said. 'I told him not to interfere.'

This wasn't true. She had said nothing.

'You ran out of the back door and disappeared for almost an hour,' I protested. 'Then you arrived with a hard-looking fellow who laughed in Joe's face.'

'A hard-looking fellow,' she repeated, as if tasting the sound of the words.

'Well, wasn't he? Where on earth did you meet him, Ellen?'

'On the train,' she answered. Immediately she seemed to regret this admission. 'You'd better not interfere in things that don't concern you, Eddie. You see what happened to Joe.'

I was amazed. She sat beside me, looking so beautiful, and talked like that.

'But that man's no good,' I cried. 'A girl isn't safe with him. He used brass knuckles on Joe – brass knuckles!'

'Is that bad?'

She asked this like a little girl. She looked at me and really wanted an answer. For a moment it seemed as if she was trying to recapture an innocence that had almost gone. Then she hardened again. I say 'hardened' because I noticed that when she was concerned with this man, her eyelids fell a little, shutting everything else out.

It was a good moment to say something, I suppose. But in spite of everything I couldn't attack her. I was too impressed by her beauty and its success. I even began to find excuses for her. Perhaps that man wasn't what he seemed to be. Perhaps – more romantically – she was involved with him against her wishes. People began to drift into the room and we couldn't talk any more, so we went in to the dance. After a while I saw Joe Jelke sitting in a corner with a bandage over one eye. He was watching Ellen as if she herself had knocked him down. I didn't go to him. I felt strange – the way I feel when I wake after sleeping through an afternoon, as if something had happened while I was asleep.

The party continued until the early hours, and all the time I watched Ellen moving among the guests. I watched her with an indefinable sense of fear until the last sleepy groups had crowded into the lifts and then drifted out into the clear, dry Minnesota night.

2

There is a middle part of our city which lies between the big houses on the hill and the business district down near the river. It is not a clearly defined area and is broken into odd, complicated shapes by streets and alleys. There are names like Seven Corners. There are not many people who could draw an accurate map of the area, though everybody travelled through it by bus or car or on foot twice a day. And although it was a busy part of town, I couldn't say what business went on there. There was a big cinema and many small ones with large **posters**. There were small shops with curious advertisements in the windows, and cigarettes and sweets inside. And on one side of a certain dark street women stood in doorways, offering their services to the men that walked past. And all through the district there were money-lenders, cheap jewellers and small clubs and bars.

The morning after the party I woke up late, feeling lazy. I had the happy feeling that for another day or two there were no classes – nothing to do except wait for another party tonight. It was a fine, bright morning and the events of last night seemed far away. After lunch I set out to walk into town. It was snowing lightly. I was about halfway through that middle part of town when suddenly I began thinking of Ellen Baker. I began worrying about her more than I had ever worried about anything before. I was tempted to go back up the hill and find her and talk to her.

It was four o'clock on a December afternoon when it is not yet dark but the street lamps are just going on. I passed a bar with a few men standing around near the door. As I went past, thinking hard of Ellen, one of them called to me, not by name, but obviously referring to me. I turned around. There was the scarred, thin-faced man who had hit Joe Jelke. He was standing in the group, looking at me with the same unpleasant smile on his face as the night before.

He was wearing a black coat, buttoned up to the neck as if he was cold. His hands were deep in his pockets and he had a **bowler hat** on his head. I was surprised, and for a moment I hesitated. But above all I was angry. Knowing that I was quicker with my hands than Joe Jelke, I took a step back in his direction. The other men weren't looking at me – I don't think they even saw me. But I knew that this one recognized me.

'Here I am. What are you going to do about it?' his eyes seemed to say.

I took another step towards him and he laughed soundlessly with that twisted smile and moved back into the group. I followed. I wanted to speak to him, although I wasn't sure what I was going to say. But when I approached the group, he had disappeared.

'Did he go inside?' I asked.

There was a short silence, and they looked at one another quickly. Then one of them said:

'Did who go inside?'

'I don't know his name.'

Another quick look passed between them. Annoyed and determined, I walked past them and into the bar. There were a few people at a lunch counter along one side and a few more playing cards. But he was not among them.

I went up to the man at the food counter.

'Did you see that fellow who just walked in here?'

He shook his head. Was he pretending to know nothing, or was it my imagination?

'What fellow?'

'Thin face – bowler hat.'

He shook his head again. 'I didn't see him,' he said.

I waited. The three men from outside had come in and were standing at the counter beside me, looking at me in a peculiar way. Feeling helpless and increasingly uneasy, I turned suddenly and went out. A little way down the street I turned again and took a good look at the place, so I'd know it and could find it again. On the next corner I started to run, found a taxi in front of the hotel and drove back up the hill.

♦ ♦ ♦ ♦

Ellen wasn't home. Mrs Baker came downstairs and talked to me. She seemed cheerful and obviously knew nothing about the events of the night before. She said she was glad I had come because Ellen would want to see me, and there was so little time. Ellen was going back to New York at half past eight tonight.

'Tonight!' I said. 'I thought she was going back the day after tomorrow.'

'She's going to visit the Brokaws in Chicago first, and then she'll go on to New York,' Mrs Baker said. 'They want her for some party. We just decided it today. She's leaving with the Ingersoll girls tonight.'

I was so glad. Ellen was safe. I had been worrying unnecessarily. This business with the thin-faced fellow had been a short adventure, nothing more, and now she was going to leave him far behind. I felt like an idiot, but I realized how much I cared about Ellen.

'Will she be in soon?'

'Any minute now. She just phoned from the University Club.'

I lived almost next door, so I said I'd come back later. When I got outside, I decided to take a shorter route which we used to take in childhood – through the Baker's back garden. It was still snowing. Trying to find the path, I noticed that the Bakers' back door was slightly open.

I hardly know why I turned and walked into that kitchen. The Bakers' servants knew me, and there was a sudden silence as I walked in. They began to work quickly, making unnecessary movements and noise. One young girl looked at me in a frightened way, and I guessed that she was waiting to deliver another message. I spoke to her.

'I know all about this,' I said. 'It's a very serious business.

55

Shall I go to Mrs Baker now, or will you shut and lock that back door?'

'Don't tell Mrs Baker, Mr Stinson!'

'Then do as I say. If you trouble Miss Ellen——' I made some improbable threat about going to all the employment offices and making sure she never got another job in the city. She was thoroughly frightened. When I went out, the back door was shut and locked behind me.

At the same time I heard a big car arrive in front of the house. It was bringing Ellen home, and I went in to say good-bye.

Joe Jelke and two other boys were there. Evidently Joe had forgiven her, or at least he was too much in love to remember last night. But I saw that, although she laughed a lot, Ellen wasn't really paying any attention to him or any of them. She wanted them to go, so that there'd be a message from the kitchen, but I knew that the message wouldn't come. She was safe. I left and walked home, feeling slightly depressed. I lay for an hour in a hot bath, thinking that the holiday was now over for me because Ellen was gone. I felt even more deeply than yesterday that she had moved out of my life.

And there was something else – something I'd forgotten. It was something to do with Mrs Baker. Now I seemed to remember that I had first thought of it during my conversation with her. I'd forgotten to ask her a question.

The Brokaws – that was it. Ellen was going to visit the Brokaws in Chicago, Mrs Baker had said. I knew Bill Brokaw well; he was in my class at Yale. Then I remembered with a shock – the Brokaws weren't in Chicago this Christmas; they were at Palm Beach!

I leapt out of the bath, threw a towel around my shoulders and ran to the phone. A servant answered; Miss Ellen had already left for the station.

Luckily our car was in and the driver brought it round to the door. The night was cold and dry and we drove quickly to the station through the snow. This business was wrong – all wrong. I dropped any idea that it was harmless. I was the only person that stood between Ellen and some unknown disaster. Or else it was the police and public shame. There was something dark and frightening here, and I didn't want Ellen to go through it alone.

There are three trains from St Paul to Chicago that all leave here at around half past eight. She was travelling on the Burlington. As I ran across the station, I saw that the Burlington had just left. But I knew that she was together with the Ingersoll girls, so she was safe until tomorrow.

I managed to catch one of the other two trains. However, I knew that Ellen would arrive in Chicago ten minutes before me. She would have ten minutes – more than enough time to disappear into one of the largest cities in the world.

At eight o'clock the next morning I pushed violently past a line of passengers and jumped out of the train onto the platform. For a moment the confusion of the great station, the sounds and echoes and bells and smoke left me helpless. Then I ran towards the exit; it was the only chance I knew.

I had guessed right. She was standing at a counter, sending off a telegram to her mother. Heaven knows what black lie she had written. Her expression when she saw me was one of terror mixed with surprise. She was thinking quickly. She would have liked to walk away from me as if I weren't there, but she couldn't. So we stood silently watching each other and each thinking hard.

'The Brokaws are in Florida,' I said after a minute.

'It was nice of you to take such a long trip to tell me that.'

'Well, you know it now, so don't you think you'd better go on to school?'

'Please leave me alone, Eddie,' she said.

'I'll go as far as New York with you. I've decided to go back early too.'

'You'd better leave me alone.' Her lovely eyes narrowed and her face had a look of refusal. Then suddenly her expression changed and she gave a cheerful smile that almost persuaded me.

'Eddie, you silly child. Don't you think I'm old enough to look after myself?' I didn't answer. 'I'm going to meet a man, you understand. I just want to see him today. I've got my ticket to go East on the five o'clock train. If you don't believe me, here it is in my bag.'

'I believe you.'

'You don't know this man, and – honestly, I think you're being awfully interfering and impossible.'

'I know who the man is.'

Again she lost control of her face. That terrible expression returned and she spoke almost fiercely:

'You'd better leave me alone.'

I took the telegram she had written out of her hand and wrote another one, explaining things to her mother. Then I turned to Ellen and said a little roughly:

'We'll take the five o'clock train East together. Until then you're going to spend the day with me.'

The sound of my own voice saying this so firmly encouraged me, and I think it impressed her too. Anyway, she followed without protest while I bought my ticket.

When I start to piece together in my mind the events of that day, a sort of confusion begins. It is as if my consciousness didn't want to let any of it pass through. It was a bright morning. I remember driving about in a taxi and going to various large shops where Ellen tried to escape from me. As we drove along Lake Shore Drive I had the feeling that someone was following us in a taxi. I tried to see them by turning round quickly or looking suddenly into the driver's mirror. But there was no one, and when I turned back, I could see that Ellen's face was twisted with cold, unnatural laughter.

All morning there was an icy wind from the lake, but while we were having lunch in a restaurant by the shore, a light snow began to fall, and we talked almost naturally about our friends, and about little things. Suddenly her voice changed; she grew serious and looked me in the eye, straight and sincere.

'Eddie, you're the oldest friend I have,' she said, 'and you should be able to trust me. If I promise you faithfully that I'll catch that five o'clock train, will you leave me alone for a few hours this afternoon?'

'Why?'

'Well——' she hesitated and hung her head a little, 'I suppose everybody has a right to say – goodbye.'

'You want to say goodbye to that——'

'Yes, yes,' she said quickly, 'just a few hours, Eddie, and I promise faithfully that I'll be on that train.'

'Well, I suppose nothing much can happen in a couple of hours. If you really want to say goodbye——'

I looked up suddenly, and saw a look of such fierceness in her face that I was shocked. Her lip was curled up and her eyes were narrow. There wasn't the slightest sign of fairness and sincerity in her whole face.

We argued. I refused to let her persuade me or infect me with any – well, there was evil in the air. She kept trying to make me believe that everything was all right. She was waiting for any weakness or doubt in my mind which she could use to her advantage. But she was getting tired. Two or three times she was close to tears. I almost had her – then she slipped away again.

I forced her into a taxi at four o'clock and we set off towards the station. The wind was icy again, and the people in the streets, waiting for buses, looked cold and unhappy. I tried to think how lucky we were with our comfortable lives and our comfortable homes; but all the familiar, respectable world I had known until yesterday had disappeared. We were carrying with us something that was the enemy and the opposite of all that. With a touch of alarm I wondered whether I was becoming like Ellen.

Ellen and I got on the train and found our car. We went into Ellen's **compartment**, shut the door and sat down.

'Ellen,' I said helplessly, 'You asked me to trust you. You have much more reason to trust me. Surely it would help if you told me a little.'

'I can't,' she said very low. 'I mean, there's nothing to tell.'

'You met this man on the train coming home and you fell in love with him, isn't that true?'

'I don't know.'

'He has some sort of hold over you,' I went on. 'He's trying to use you; he's trying to get something from you. He's not in love with you.'

'What does that matter?' she said in a weak voice.

'It does matter. Instead of trying to fight this thing, you're fighting me. And I love you Ellen. Do you hear? I'm telling you this for the first time now, but it isn't new with me. I love you.'

She looked at me with an unpleasant smile on her gentle face.

'Ellen, I want you to answer one question. Is he going to be on this train?'

She hesitated. At that moment I knew without any doubt that he was just outside the door. She knew it, too, and turned pale. I held my head in my hands and tried to think.

We must have sat there without a word for more than an hour. I was conscious that the lights of Chicago were moving past. Then we were out on the dark flatness of Illinois.

After a while I persuaded myself that I was strong enough – that my faith in people and things was strong enough – for the struggle that was coming. I had no doubt that this person's purpose was criminal, but there wasn't any reason to believe that he had more than human intelligence. He was a man. But I suppose I already half knew what I would find when I opened the door.

When I stood up, Ellen didn't seem to see me at all. She was curled up in a corner, staring into space. I knelt beside her and kissed her two hands. Then I opened the door and went out into the corridor.

I closed the door behind me. The corridor was dark except for the two lights at each end. A man was standing further down the car outside the men's smoking-room. His collar was turned up, as if he was cold, and he was wearing a bowler hat. When I saw him, he turned and went into the smoking-room, and I followed. He was sitting in the far corner on the long leather seat; I sat in the single armchair by the door.

As I went in I nodded to him and he gave one of those terrible, soundless laughs. But this time the laugh seemed to go on forever. Mainly in order to cut it short, I asked: 'Where are you from?'

He stopped laughing and looked at me through narrow eyes. When he decided to answer, his voice seemed to come from a great distance.

'I'm from St Paul, Jack.'

'Have you been making a trip home?'

He nodded. Then he took a long breath and spoke in a loud, threatening voice:

The corridor was dark except for two lights at each end. A man was standing there, outside the men's smoking room.

'You'd better get off at the next station, Jack.'

He was dead. He was as dead as hell – he had been dead all this time. The force that gave him a sort of life, the force that had carried him out to St Paul and back, was leaving him now. Another figure was becoming visible behind the solid shape of the man on the seat opposite me – it was the figure of a dead man.

He spoke again with difficulty.

'You get off at Fort Wayne, Jack, or I'm going to finish you.' He moved his hand in his coat pocket, and I saw that he had a gun.

I shook my head. 'You can't touch me,' I answered. 'You see, I know.'

His terrible eyes moved quickly, trying to guess whether or not I did know. Then he gave a noise like a wild animal and seemed to be about to jump to his feet.

'You climb off here or else I'm going to get you, Jack!' he said fiercely. The train was slowing as it approached Fort Wayne. His voice was loud in the stillness, but he didn't move from his chair – he was too weak, I think. No one got into our car. After a while the train slid out of the station and into the long darkness.

I remember the next five or six hours as if they were a dream. It must have been five or six hours, but looking back now it seems like something outside time – five minutes or a year, I cannot say. There was a slow, purposeful attack on me, wordless and terrible. I felt a strangeness take hold of me – like the strangeness I had felt all afternoon, but deeper and stronger. It was like the sensation of drifting away. I gripped the arms of the chair, as if to hold on to a piece of the living world. Sometimes I almost lost consciousness. I almost looked forward to it and was tempted to let go. Then, with desperate willpower, I pulled myself back.

Suddenly I realized that I had stopped hating him. I didn't feel he was a stranger any more. I went cold and started to sweat. He was beginning to work on my feelings. He had won control of Ellen in the same way.

He must have seen my hesitation because he spoke in a low, steady, almost gentle voice: 'You'd better go now.'

'Oh, I'm not going,' I forced myself to say.

'Whatever you say, Jack.'

'What do you want from this girl?' I said in a shaking voice. 'You want to turn her life into a walking hell, is that it?'

His eyes showed surprise, as if I had accused him unfairly. I went on blindly: 'You've lost her; she's put her trust in me.'

His face went suddenly black with evil, and he cried: 'You're a liar!' His voice was like cold hands at my throat.

'She trusts me,' I said. 'You can't touch her, she's safe.'

He controlled himself. His face grew calm and I felt that strange weakness begin again inside me. A feeling of hopelessness came over me.

'You haven't got much time left,' I forced myself to say. Then I suddenly guessed the truth. 'You died, or you were killed, not far from here!' – Then I saw something I had not noticed before. There was a small round bullet hole in the middle of his head. 'And now you're sinking. You've only got a few hours. The trip home is over!'

His face was suddenly as ugly as hell. It was not human, neither living nor dead. At the same time the room was full of cold air and there was a sound of horrible laughter. He was on his feet.

'Come and look!' he cried. 'I'll show you——'

He took a step towards me and it was as if a door had opened behind him – a door which opened onto unimaginable darkness and evil. There was a scream of pain and suddenly the breath went out of him in a long sigh and he sank to the floor . . .

I don't know how long I sat there in terror and exhaustion. The next thing I remember is our arrival at Pittsburgh. There was something lying on the seat opposite me – something too pale to be a man, too dark and heavy to be a shadow. While I watched it, it slowly disappeared.

Some minutes later I opened the door of Ellen's compartment. She was asleep where I had left her. Her lovely cheeks were white, but her breathing was regular and clear. The thing that had taken control of her was gone and she was exhausted, but she was herself again.

I laid a blanket over her, turned off the light and went out.

3

When I came home for the Easter holiday, I went straight down to the bar at Seven Corners. The barman naturally didn't remember my visit three months before.

'I'm trying to find a certain person who used to come here a lot some time ago.'

I described the man accurately. When I had finished, the barman called to a little fellow who was sitting at one of the tables.

'Hey, Shorty, talk to this fellow, will you? I think he's looking for Joe Varland.'

The little man gave me a slow look. I went and sat near him.

'Joe Varland's dead' he said. 'He died last winter.'

I described him again – his coat, his laugh, the habitual expression of his eyes.

'That's Joe Varland alright, but he's dead.'

'I want to find out something about him.'

'What do you want to find out?'

'What did he do, for example?'

'How should I know?'

'Look, I'm not a policeman. I just want some information about his habits. He's dead now and it can't hurt him. And I won't pass on the information.'

'Well' – he hesitated, looking at me closely – 'he travelled a lot on trains. He got into an argument in the station in Pittsburg and a policeman shot him.'

I nodded. Broken pieces of the puzzle were beginning to fall into place.

'Why was he a lot on trains?'

'How should I know?'

'If you can use ten dollars, I'd like to know anything you've heard about the subject.'

'Well,' said Shorty, 'I only know that they used to say he worked the trains.'

'What do you mean "worked the trains"?'

'He had some business of his own which he never talked about. He used to get money from girls who travelled alone on trains. Nobody ever knew much about it – he didn't talk about it. But sometimes he came here with a lot of money, and we knew he got it from the girls he met on trains.'

I thanked him and gave him the ten dollars. I went out, thinking deeply.

Ellen didn't come West at Easter, and even if she had come, I wouldn't have gone to her with the information. But at least I've seen her almost every day this summer and we've managed to talk about everything else. Sometimes, though, she gets silent and wants to be very close to me, and I know what's in her mind.

She's finishing school in New York this autumn and coming back to St Paul, while I have two more years at New

Haven. But things don't look as impossible as they did a few months ago. She belongs to me – even if I lose her, she belongs to me. Who knows? Anyway, I'll always be there.

THE BRIDAL PARTY

1

There was the usual insincere little note saying: 'I wanted you to be the first to know.' Michael was shocked. She was getting married, and the wedding was going to be held not in New York, far away, but here in Paris right under his nose. The date was only two weeks off, early in June.

At first Michael was afraid and his stomach felt hollow. He left the hotel and wandered around the streets, but the fear stayed with him. After a while he recognized it as the fear that now he would never be happy. He had met Caroline Dandy in New York when she was seventeen. He had won her young heart and kept it for a year. Then he had lost her, slowly, tragically, uselessly, because he had no money and could make no money. He had lost her because he could not find himself. Although she still loved him, Caroline had begun to pity him. She had begun to see a future for herself which he could never share.

His only hope was that she loved him, and he held on to it desperately. But the hope became an empty dream, and he left for France. He carried the memories around with him in Paris in the form of photographs and packets of letters and a liking for a popular song called 'Among My Souvenirs'. He avoided other girls, as if Caroline would know it and be faithful like him. Her note informed him that he had lost her for ever.

It was a fine morning. In front of the shops in the rue de Castiglione people were standing looking upwards. Far above, the Graf Zeppelin, shining and beautiful, was sailing across the Paris sky. He heard a woman say in French that it would not surprise her if that thing started to drop bombs. Then he heard another, familiar voice, full of laughter, and the hollow in his stomach froze. Turning suddenly, he was face to face with Caroline Dandy and her future husband.

'Why, Michael! We've been trying to contact you.'

Why didn't they just walk away, Michael thought. He imagined them walking backwards down the rue de Castiglione, across the rue de Rivoli and through the Tuileries Gardens till they disappeared completely across the river.

'This is Hamilton Rutherford.'

'We've met before.'

'At Pat's, wasn't it?'

'And last spring in the Ritz Bar.'

'Michael, where have you been all this time?'

'Around here.' This was too painful. He remembered things he had heard about Hamilton Rutherford. He knew that he had made a lot of money working in Wall Street. He was not handsome like Michael, but strong and attractive, confident, just the right height for Caroline, while Michael had always been too short for her when they danced.

Rutherford was saying: 'No, I'd like it very much if you'd come to the **bachelor** dinner. I've booked the Ritz Bar from nine o'clock on. Then right after the wedding there'll be a reception and breakfast at the Hôtel Georges-Cinq.'

'And, Michael, George Packman is giving a party the day after tomorrow at Chez Victor, and I want you to come. And also to tea at Jebby West's on Friday; she'd love to see you. Where's your hotel so we can send you an invitation? You see, the reason we decided to have the wedding over

Turning suddenly, he was face to face with Caroline Dandy and her future husband.

here is because Mother has been sick in a nursing home here and the whole family is in Paris. And Hamilton's mother is here too——'

The whole family; they had always hated him, except her mother. They had always discouraged his interest in Caroline. How unimportant he was in this game of families and money! He began to make excuses.

Then it happened – Caroline saw deep into him. She saw through to his wounded heart, and something inside her reacted. He saw the emotion in the curve of her mouth and in her eyes. He had moved her. Their hearts had in some way touched across two feet of Paris sunlight. She took her fiancé's arm suddenly, as if to steady herself.

They said goodbye. Michael walked quickly for a minute; then he stopped, pretending to look in a window. He saw them further up the street, walking fast into the Place Vendôme, people with a lot to do.

He had things to do also – he had to get his laundry.

'Nothing will ever be the same again,' he said to himself. 'She will never be happy in her marriage and I will never be happy at all any more.'

The two years of his love for Caroline filled his thoughts. Memories came back to him – of rides in the Long Island moonlight; of a happy time at Lake Placid; of a terrible afternoon in a little café on Forty-eighth Street in the last sad months when their marriage finally seemed impossible.

Back at the hotel there was a telegram for Michael. In it he read that his grandfather had died, leaving him a quarter of a million dollars. 'If I'd known this a month ago——' he thought. 'But it's too late now.' After the first excitement, his unhappiness was greater than ever. He lay awake in bed, thinking of the look in Caroline's eyes that morning – the look that seemed to say: 'Oh, why weren't you stronger?

Why didn't you make me marry you? Don't you see how sad I am?'

Michael gripped the side of his bed.

'Well, I won't lose hope till the last moment,' he whispered. 'I've had all the bad luck up till now, but maybe my luck has changed at last. You have to fight for what you want. And if I can't have her, at least she'll go into this marriage with some of me in her heart.'

2

With this new determination he went to the party at Chez Victor two days later. He was early; the only other person in the bar was a tall, handsome man of about fifty. They spoke.

'You waiting for George Packman's party?'

'Yes. My name's Michael Curly.'

'My name's——'

Michael didn't hear the name. They ordered a drink, and Michael commented that the **bride** and **groom** were probably having a lively time.

'Too much so,' the other man agreed unenthusiastically. 'I don't know how they do it. We all crossed on the boat together; five days of that crazy life and then two weeks of Paris. You' – he hesitated, smiling slightly – 'You'll excuse me for saying that your generation drinks too much. Hamilton drinks too much, and all this crowd of young people drink too much. Do you live in Paris?'

'For the moment.' said Michael.

'I don't like Paris. My wife – that is to say, my ex-wife, Hamilton's mother – lives in Paris.'

'You're Hamilton Rutherford's father?'

'Yes. And I'm not denying that I'm proud of what he's done. I was just talking about young people in general.'

'Of course.'

Michael looked up as four people came in. He felt suddenly that his dinner coat was old and shiny; he had ordered a new one that morning. The people who had come in were rich and sure of themselves. When Caroline arrived, Michael hardly had time to talk to her. He could see that, like the others, she was tired. She was pale and there were shadows under her eyes. Michael was half glad, half disappointed when he was placed at another table far from her. He looked around at the other guests. They were not like the young people he and Caroline had known; the men were more than thirty and successful. Next to him was Jebby West, whom he knew. On his left was a man who laughed a lot and immediately began to talk to Michael. He was planning a practical joke for the bachelor dinner – they were going to hire a French girl who would appear in the middle of the dinner with a real baby in her arms, crying: 'Hamilton, you can't leave me now!' The idea seemed unamusing to Michael, but his table companion was thoroughly pleased with it.

Further up the table there was talk of the financial crisis – another fall in the market today, the biggest since 1929. People were joking to Rutherford about it: 'Too bad, old man. You'd better not get married, after all.'

Michael asked the man on his left, 'Has he lost a lot?'

'Nobody knows. He's heavily involved, but he's one of the cleverest young men in Wall Street. Anyway, nobody ever tells you the truth.'

It was a **champagne** dinner from the start, and towards the end it became pleasantly lively. But Michael saw that all these people were too exhausted to enjoy themselves naturally. For weeks they had drunk **cocktails** before meals like Americans, wines like Frenchmen, beer like Germans. They were no longer in their twenties, and this unhealthy mixture helped only to make them less conscious of the mistakes of the night before. The only people who seemed really lively were those who drank nothing.

But Michael was not tired, and the champagne gave him confidence. He had been away from New York for more than eight months and most of the dance music was unfamiliar to him, but hearing a tune he knew, he crossed to Caroline's table and asked her to dance.

She was lovely in a dress of heavenly blue, and the nearness of her yellow hair, of her cool and tender grey eyes, made him dance badly. For a moment it seemed there was nothing to say. He wanted to tell her about his grandfather's money, but he didn't know how to start.

'Michael, it's so nice to be dancing with you again.'

He forced a smile.

'I'm so happy that you came,' she continued. 'I was afraid maybe you'd be silly and stay away. Now we can be just good friends and natural together. Michael, I want you and Hamilton to like each other.'

'I could kill him without hesitation,' he said pleasantly, 'but he looks like a good man. He's fine. But tell me, what happens to people like me who aren't able to forget?'

As he said this he could not hide the emotion in his voice. Caroline gave him a quick look and her heart opened, as it had the other morning.

'Does it upset you so much, Michael?'

'Yes.'

His voice seemed to come up from his shoes. For a second they were not dancing; they were simply holding on to one another. Then she turned away from him and twisted her mouth into a lovely smile.

'I didn't know what to do at first, Michael. I told Hamilton about you, but it didn't worry him, and he was right. Because I've recovered now – yes, I have. And you'll wake up some sunny morning and you'll realize that you have recovered too.'

He shook his head stubbornly.

'Oh, yes. We weren't made for each other. I need some-body like Hamilton to decide things. It was that more than the question of – of——'

'Of money.' Again he was tempted to tell her the news, but again he decided it was not the right moment.

'Then how do you explain what happened the other day,' he demanded helplessly, – 'and what happened just now? Those moments when we just open our hearts to one another the way we used to – as if we were one person?'

'Oh, don't!' she begged him. 'You mustn't talk like that; everything's decided now. I love Hamilton with all my heart. But I still remember certain things in the past and I feel sorry for you – for us – for the way we were.'

'I've got to see you alone,' he said. 'When can I?'

'I'll be at Jebby West's tea tomorrow,' she whispered.

But he did not talk to her at Jebby West's tea. Rutherford stood next to her all evening and they shared every conversation. They left early.

Michael was desperate. Finally he took a bold step; he wrote to Hamilton Rutherford, asking him for a meeting the following afternoon. Rutherford agreed.

They were going to meet in the bar of the Hôtel Jéna. Michael prepared a speech. 'See here, Rutherford,' he would say, 'do you realize the responsibility you are taking? Do you realize what will happen if you persuade a girl into a marriage that is against the needs of her heart?' He would explain that the question of money had now been solved. And he would

74

demand that Caroline should have the chance to decide for herself before it was too late.

Rutherford would be angry; there might be a row, but Michael felt that he was fighting for his life now.

He found Rutherford talking with an older man.

'I saw what happened to most of my friends,' Rutherford was saying, 'and I decided it wasn't going to happen to me. It isn't so difficult. If you take a girl with common sense, and tell her what's what and do the right thing, it's a marriage. If you put up with any nonsense at the beginning, it won't last – either the man gets out, or the girl eats him up.'

Michael's blood boiled slowly.

'Haven't you ever thought,' he enquired coldly, 'that your ideas went out of fashion about a hundred years ago?'

'No, they didn't,' said Rutherford pleasantly, but impatiently. 'I'm as modern as anybody. I'd get married in an aeroplane next Saturday if it would please my girl.'

'I don't mean that way of being modern. You can't take a sensitive woman——'

'Sensitive? Women aren't so sensitive. It's fellows like you that are sensitive. It's fellows like you that let themselves be used by women.'

'Caroline is sensitive,' said Michael.

The other man got up to go. When they were alone, Rutherford turned to Michael.

'Caroline's more than sensitive,' he said. 'She's got sense. There aren't many men who are strong enough to take control of their marriage any more, but I intend to be one of them.'

'Do you realize the responsibility you're taking?'

'I certainly do,' interrupted Rutherford. 'I'm not afraid of responsibility. I'll make the decisions – fairly, I hope, but anyway they'll be final.'

'What if you didn't start right?' said Michael suddenly. 'What if your marriage is not built on shared love?'

'I think I see what you mean,' Rutherford said, still pleasant. 'But let me say that if you and Caroline had married, it wouldn't have lasted three years. You were sorry for each other, but that's not enough. Marriage should be built on hope.' He looked at his watch and stood up.

'I've got to meet Caroline. Remember, you're coming to the bachelor dinner the day after tomorrow.'

Michael felt the opportunity slipping away. 'Then Caroline's personal feelings don't matter to you?' he demanded fiercely.

'Caroline's tired and upset. But she has what she wants, and that's the main thing.'

'Are you referring to yourself?' demanded Michael in disbelief.

'Yes.'

'May I ask how long she's wanted you?'

'About two years.' Before Michael could answer he was gone.

During the next two days Michael drifted in an ocean of helplessness. He phoned Caroline, but she insisted that she could not possibly see him until the day before the wedding. Then he went to the bachelor dinner.

The Ritz Bar had been decorated with French and American flags. Michael felt different in his new dinner coat and his new hat. He did not feel such an outsider among all these people who were rich and confident. For the first time since he had left college he felt rich and confident himself; he felt that he was part of all this. He even agreed to help Johnson, the practical joker. The woman Johnson had hired was waiting quietly with her baby in the room across the hall.

'We don't want to overdo it,' Johnson said, 'Ham's probably had enough worries today. It's been another bad day on Wall Street. Fullman Oil is sixteen points down.'

'Is that bad news for him?' Michael asked, trying to hide his interest.

'Naturally. He's heavily involved; he's always heavily involved. He's had luck – until now, that is.'

The glasses were filled and emptied faster now, and men were shouting at one another across the narrow table.

'Now's the time,' Johnson said. 'You stand by the door, and we'll both pretend to try and stop her coming in – just long enough to get everybody's attention.'

He went out into the corridor, and Michael waited. Several minutes passed. Then Johnson reappeared with a curious expression on his face.

'There's something odd about this.'

'Isn't the girl there?'

'She's there all right, but there's another woman there, too; and it's not anybody I hired. She wants to see Hamilton Rutherford, and she looks as if she intends to make trouble.'

They went out into the hall. In a chair near the door sat an American girl who looked slightly drunk, but wore a determined expression on her face.

'Well, d'you tell him?' she demanded. 'The name is Marjorie Collins, and he'll know it. I've come a long way, and I want to see him now and quick.'

'You go in and tell Ham,' whispered Johnson to Michael. 'Maybe he'd better get out. I'll keep her here.'

Back at the dinner table Michael whispered into Rutherford's ear:

'A girl outside named Marjorie Collins says she wants to see you. I think she wants to make trouble.'

Hamilton Rutherford's mouth fell open; then slowly the

lips came together in a straight line and he said in a firm voice:

'Please keep her there. And send the head waiter to me straight away.'

Michael spoke to the head waiter. Then, without returning to the table, he asked quietly for his coat and hat. He passed Johnson and the girl in the hall without speaking and went out into the rue Cambon. He stopped a taxi and gave the driver the address of Caroline's hotel.

Michael did not want to bring her bad news; he just wanted to be with her when she needed him. Rutherford thought he was soft – well, he was hard enough, and he would take any opportunity that offered itself. If she decided to turn away from Rutherford, she would find him there.

Caroline was in; she was surprised when he called, but she came down to sit with him in the hotel lounge. She was holding two blue telegrams in her hand.

'But Michael, is the dinner over?'

'I wanted to see you, so I came away.'

'I'm glad.' Her voice was friendly, but distant. 'Maybe we can talk a little.'

'You're tired,' he guessed. 'Perhaps I should go.'

'No, I was waiting for Hamilton. There are these telegrams for him. He said he might be late, so I'm glad I have someone to talk to.'

'Doesn't it matter to you what time he gets home?'

'Naturally,' she said, laughing, 'but what can I do? I can't start telling him what he can and can't do.'

'Why not?'

'He wouldn't accept it.'

'He seems to want a housekeeper and nothing more,' said Michael in a low voice.

'Tell me about your plans, Michael,' she asked quickly.

'My plans? I can't see any future after the day after tomorrow. The only real plan I ever had was to love you.'

Their eyes met for a moment and Michael recognized that same look in Caroline's eyes. Words poured quickly from his heart:

'Let me tell you just once more how well I've loved you. I've never doubted, never thought of another girl. And now, when I think of a future without you, I don't want to live, Caroline darling. I used to dream about our home, our children, about holding you in my arms and touching your face and hands and hair. I've never stopped dreaming, and now I can't wake up.'

Caroline was crying softly. 'Poor Michael – poor Michael.' Her hand reached out and her fingers touched the sleeve of his dinner coat. 'I was so sorry for you the other night. You looked so thin and as if you needed a new coat. I thought you needed somebody to take care of you.' She looked more closely at his coat. 'Why, you've got a new suit! And a new hat! Why, Michael, how fine!' She laughed and was suddenly cheerful despite her tears.

'My grandfather left me about a quarter of a million dollars,' he said.

'Why, Michael,' she cried, 'how perfectly wonderful! I'm so glad. I've always thought you were the sort of person who ought to have money.'

'Yes, just too late to make a difference.'

The door opened and Hamilton Rutherford walked in. His eyes were restless and impatient.

'Hello, darling; hello, Mr Curly.' He bent and kissed Caroline. 'I left the dinner for a minute to find out if I had any telegrams. I see you've got them there.' He took the telegrams from her, remarking to Michael: 'That was an odd business there in the bar, wasn't it? Especially when some of you were planning a similar sort of joke yourselves.' He opened one of the telegrams, closed it and turned to Caroline.

'A girl I haven't seen for two years came to the dinner,' he said. 'It seems she wanted money, though I've never owed her anything in my life.'

'What happened?'

'The head waiter called the police and the matter was settled in five minutes. French law takes this sort of thing very seriously, and they gave the girl a fright that she'll remember. But it seems wiser to tell you.'

'Are you suggesting that I mentioned the matter?' said Michael stiffly.

'No,' Rutherford said slowly. 'No, you were just going to be available. And since you're here, I'll tell you some news that will interest you even more.'

He handed Michael one telegram and opened the other.

'What does it mean?' asked Michael.

'Together these two telegrams mean that I have to start life again.'

Michael saw Caroline's face grow a shade paler, but she sat as quiet as a mouse.

'It was a mistake and I didn't realize it soon enough,' continued Rutherford. 'So you see I don't have all the luck, Mr Curly. And that reminds me; they tell me you've received some money.'

'Yes,' said Michael.

'That's it then,' Rutherford turned to Caroline. 'You understand, darling, that I'm not joking or exaggerating. I've lost everything and I'm starting again from nothing.'

Two pairs of eyes were fixed on her – Rutherford's calm and undemanding, Michael's hungry, tragic, begging. In a minute she had risen from her chair and with a little cry thrown herself into Hamilton Rutherford's arms.

'Oh, darling,' she cried, 'what does it matter! It's better; I like it better, honestly I do! I want to start that way; I want to! Oh, please don't be sad or worry even for a minute!'

'All right, baby,' said Rutherford. His hand stroked her hair gently for a moment; then he took his arm from around her.

'I promised to join the party for an hour,' he said. 'So I'll say good night, and I want you to go to bed soon and get a good sleep. Good night, Mr Curly. I'm sorry you've become involved in all these financial matters.'

But Michael had already picked up his hat. 'I'll go along with you,' he said.

3

It was such a fine morning. Michael's new jacket hadn't been delivered, so he felt rather uncomfortable when he saw the cameras and moving-picture machines in front of the little church on the avenue Georges-Cinq. It was such a clean, new church that it seemed unforgivable not to appear properly dressed. Michael, white and shaky from the night before, decided to stand at the back. From there he looked at the back of Caroline, and the fat back of George Packman, who looked unsteady as if he wanted to support himself against the bride and groom.

Michael was standing near the door when the bride and groom began to walk back towards him between the rows of seats, followed by a line of people. He realized with alarm that everyone would see him and speak to him.

Rutherford and Caroline reached him first. Rutherford was serious and Caroline was lovelier than he had ever seen her. Michael managed to say, 'Beautiful, simply beautiful,' and then other people passed and spoke to him – old Mrs Dandy, looking well despite her illness, a very fine old lady indeed; and Rutherford's father and mother, ten years separated, but walking side by side and looking proud. Then all Caroline's sisters and their husbands and her little nephews.

He wondered what would happen now. Rutherford had sent out invitations for a party at the Georges-Cinq, an expensive place. Would Rutherford change his plans after those disastrous telegrams? It seemed not, since everyone was moving off in the direction of the hotel in colourful groups. With their long dresses the girls were like flowers in the bright June sunlight.

Michael needed a drink. He went through a side entrance to the hotel and asked for the bar. But – how did it happen? – the bar was full. There was already a small crowd of men and women from the wedding, all needing a drink. Cocktails and champagne were served – Rutherford's cocktails and champagne. He had hired the whole bar and hall and the two great reception rooms and all the stairs between the floors, and windows looking out over Paris. Eventually, Michael went and joined the line of guests who were waiting to congratulate the bridal party. He listened to the voices around him: 'Such a lovely wedding'; 'My dear, you were simply lovely'; 'You're a lucky man, Rutherford.' When Michael came to Caroline, she took a single step forward and kissed him on the lips, but he felt no contact in the kiss – it was unreal; and he continued along the line. Old Mrs Dandy held his hand for a minute and thanked him for the flowers he had sent when she was ill.

'I'm sorry I haven't written; you know, we old ladies are grateful for——' Michael saw that all this – the flowers, the fact that she had not written, the wedding – all this was equally important or unimportant to her. She had married off five other children and she had seen two of those marriages break up. To her this whole thing was just a familiar show which she had seen many times before.

Waiters were already serving a lunch with champagne at small tables and there was music. Michael sat down with Jebby West. 'Wasn't Caroline lovely?' Jebby West said. 'So perfectly calm. I asked her this morning if she was at all nervous, and she said "Why should I be? I've wanted him for two years, and now I'm just happy, that's all."'

'It must be true,' said Michael gloomily.

'What?'

'What you just said.'

He had been wounded, but he felt nothing.

He asked Jebby to dance. An hour or so later Michael realized suddenly that it was afternoon. In one corner of the hall photographers were taking official pictures of the bride and groom. Still as death and pale under the bright lights, they appeared like wax models.

After the bridal party had been photographed, pictures were taken of the families and children. Later, Caroline, active and excited, came and caught Michael by the sleeve.

'Now we'll have some pictures taken of just old friends.' Her voice suggested that this was the best friend of all. 'Come here – Jebby, George – not you, Hamilton; this is just my friends – Sally——'

A little while after that, the party became wilder and the hours floated past on a steady stream of champagne. In the modern fashion, Hamilton Rutherford sat at the table with his arm around an old girl of his. He told his guests, including a few alarmed but enthusiastic Europeans, that the party was not over yet; they were all going to meet at Zelli's after midnight.

'It's amazing,' George Packman was telling Michael

83

enthusiastically. 'This party will cost Ham about five thousand dollars, and that's about all the money he has in the world. But did he change any of the arrangements? Not he! He's got something special, that young man. Do you know T. G. Vance offered him a job at fifty thousand dollars a year ten minutes before the wedding this morning? In another year he'll be back with the millionaires.'

The conversation was interrupted by a plan to carry Rutherford out on the shoulders of half a dozen of his friends. After that they stood in the four o'clock sunshine waving goodbye to the bride and groom. But there must have been a mistake somewhere because five minutes later Michael saw both bride and groom coming down the stairs to the reception, each with a glass of champagne held high.

'This is our way of doing things,' he thought. 'Generous and fresh and free, but at a more nervous speed nowadays.'

Standing in the middle of the room, he realized suddenly that he hadn't really thought of Caroline for hours. He looked around with a sort of alarm, and then he saw her across the room, very bright and young and happy. He saw Rutherford near her, looking at her as if he could never look long enough. And as Michael watched them, they seemed to drift away into a future of their own, just as he had imagined that day in the rue de Castiglione. Soon they were so far away that he could hardly see them.

Michael was free again. The wedding had been for him an introduction into a new life, leaving old regrets behind. All the bitterness went out of him and the world appeared fresh and new in the spring sunshine. He had arranged to have dinner tonight with one of the girls at the wedding, but he couldn't remember which one. He was still trying to remember as he walked forward to wish Hamilton and Caroline Rutherford goodbye.

Five minutes later, the bride and groom came down the stairs to the reception, each with a glass of champagne held high.

ABOUT F. SCOTT FITZGERALD

When Fitzgerald's first novel, *This Side of Paradise*, was published in 1920, it met with almost immediate success, and its author was greeted as the poet of a new post-war generation which did not share the ideals and beliefs of its parents. Fitzgerald described his view of American life in a series of novels and short stories, written through the 1920s and 1930s, working briefly in Hollywood, the home of the 'American dream'. However, his early popularity was short-lived, and he often saw himself as a failure both as a person and as a writer.

Francis Scott Fitzgerald was born in 1896 in St Paul, Minnesota. He began writing at school, and later neglected his studies at Princeton University in order to follow his literary interests. He left Princeton before graduating to join the army. It was while he was in the army that he met Zelda Sayre, who later became his wife. Fitzgerald's early success enabled the young couple to share for a while, first in New York and later in Europe, the brilliant lifestyle which characterized the 'golden youth' of the 1920s, the 'Jazz Age'. However, financial problems, Fitzgerald's drinking and Zelda's mental illness made their life together a story of unhappiness and disasters. Fitzgerald died of a heart attack in December 1940 at the age of forty-four.

Among his works are the novels *The Great Gatsby* (1925) and *Tender is the Night* (1934). His final novel, *The Last Tycoon*, was left unfinished at his death. He also produced several collections of short stories, including *Tales of the Jazz Age* (1922) and *All the Sad Young Men* (1926). Fitzgerald used some of his personal crises in a book of short stories called *The Crack-Up* (1945).

Bernice Bobs her Hair

Comprehension

Read these sentences about Bernice. Each one comes in a
different section of the story. Number the sentences in the
order they appear in the story.

[1] Men did not talk to her about kissable mouths.

[ ] It was ugly – she had known it would be ugly.

[ ] 'You've got to learn to be nice to men who are not
successful with girls.'

[ ] 'She's absolutely hopeless!'

[ ] Behind her back they would all laugh and know that
Marjorie had made a fool of her.

[ ] Yes, she was pretty, definitely pretty; and tonight her
face was lively and excited.

Can you find a good title for each of the six sections of the story?

Discussion

1 Which of the two girls, Bernice or Marjorie, do you
sympathize and agree with most? Why?
2 What do you think would be the modern equivalent of
bobbed hair?

Review

1   Do you think it would be possible to rewrite this story in a modern context?
2   In what ways are young people different nowadays?

The Baby Party

Comprehension

Edith Andros later tells a friend about what happened at the Markeys' house that evening. Her version of events is not completely accurate. Retell this part of the story accurately. This is what she says:

'It took me a while to get little Ede washed and dressed, so we arrived at the party a bit late. Everything was fine until little Billy Markey started to show off with his new teddy-bear (you know how spoilt he is!). Ede wanted to have a look at the teddy, but Billy wouldn't let her come near, so she ran after him. Of course, the boy's so fat, he fell flat on his face and started screaming as if he'd hurt himself. I tried to help, but Mrs Markey wouldn't let me. She said it was little Ede's fault and said she was going to punish her. Can you believe it? Poor little Ede was in tears by now, but when I tried to say something, that Markey woman just started insulting me. So I decided it was time to go and I got my coat. But then Joe Markey arrived and started threatening me. They were literally pushing me out of the house, when John arrived . . .'

Discussion

'John Andros knew at last what he had fought for so wildly
that evening. He had it now, he would keep it for ever . . .'
(p. 46)

What do you think John Andros discovers at the end of
the story?

A Short Trip Home

Comprehension

What age are the main characters in this story (Eddie,
Ellen, Joe Jalke, Joe Varland)? What are the details in the
story which tell us this?

Writing

We see everything that happens in this story through the
eyes of Eddie. Consider how Ellen might have seen the
same events and write a short account of what happened
from her point of view.

Review

'This is a kind of horror story.' Do you agree? What are the
usual ingredients of a horror story? Which of those
ingredients are in this story? Do you know any other stories
with similar characters and situations?

89

The Bridal Party

Comprehension

Look at the names of the places in the box. Write the names of the places in the order they come in the story and next to each name say what happened at each place.

> Jebby West's   Caroline's hotel   the Ritz Bar
> Chez Victor   the church on the Avenue Georges-Cinq
> Hôtel Georges-Cinq   rue de Castiglione
> Hôtel Jéna   Michael's hotel

Place	What happened there
Example: rue de Castiglione	Michael met Caroline and Hamilton by accident in the street.
1	
2	
3	
4	
5	
6	
7	
8	

Discussion

Why does Caroline choose Hamilton Rutherford instead of Michael? Do you think she makes the right choice?

Writing

Write short descriptions of Hamilton and Michael. Describe
their appearance, their personality, their opinions, their
ambitions. Use any evidence you can find in the story.

All Four Stories

Review

Which of the four stories did you enjoy most? Which did you
enjoy least? Why? If you wanted to make a film of one of
these four stories, which one would you choose and why?